FEAR IS JUST A FOUR-LETTER WORD

FEAR IS JUST A FOUR-LETTER WORD

HOW TO DEVELOP THE UNSTOPPABLE CONFIDENCE TO OWN ANY ROOM

Tracy Tutor

PORTFOLIO / PENGUIN

PORTFOLIO / PENGUIN
An imprint of Penguin Random House LLC
penguinrandomhouse.com

Most Portfolio books are available at a discount when purchased in quantity for sales promotions or corporate use. Special editions, which include personalized covers, excerpts, and corporate imprints, can be created when purchased in large quantities. For more information, please call (212) 572-2232 or e-mail specialmarkets@penguinrandomhouse.com. Your local bookstore can also assist with discounted bulk purchases using the Penguin Random House corporate Business-to-Business program. For assistance in locating a participating retailer, e-mail B2B@penguinrandomhouse.com.

ISBN 9780593188736 (hardcover)
ISBN 9780593188743 (ebook)

Printed in the United States of America
1   3   5   7   9   10   8   6   4   2

Book design by Nicole LaRoche

Some names and identifying details have been changed
to protect the privacy of the individuals involved.

While the author has made every effort to provide accurate telephone numbers, internet addresses, and other contact information at the time of publication, neither the publisher nor the author assumes any responsibility for errors or for changes that occur after publication. Further, the publisher does not have any control over and does not assume any responsibility for author or third-party websites or their content.

*To every female out there waiting for
the right moment to make a move . . . the time is now.*

**YOU HAVE A LOT OF MOTHERFUCKERS
TO PROVE WRONG.**

Contents

Introduction

....

Have you ever felt like you had no control of a situation, because you were so scared of someone sitting across from you? Or felt paralyzed by the idea of what might happen if you say or do what you really feel? Fear is such a bitch, and totally to blame when this happens. As you know, it can be both commanding and terrifying, and it's normally brought on (for me, at least) by stepping into rooms that I've never been in before. They're full of huge personality types that seem impossible to get a handle on. My life as one of the top real estate brokers in Los Angeles is full of fast-talking, out-of-control egos that think they know more than I do. They're the kind of personalities that will do anything to get exactly what they want when they want it and have no problem trying to steamroll or undercut me while they're at it.

Maybe I attract more crazy than most, but in the last three seasons starring as the first female agent on *Million Dollar Listing Los Angeles*, it's clear that using quick wit and fearless responses to constantly challenge the (mostly) men around me has resonated, especially with other women. I'm known for being both tough and totally vulnerable, and for using a "no bullshit" attitude wrapped in some humor to get exactly what I want. I'm never anything other than 100 percent myself, which comes through as much in the show as it does in my daily life. Knowing which part of my personality to bring to every situation—the feminine side, the sincere one, the humor, the straightforward questions—gives me a lot to work with in figuring out how to own each room and each personality that I'm faced with.

If you're thinking that having "total control" of both yourself and the situations you find yourself in seems pretty far off right now, don't worry. Yes, the people you're dealing with seem scary, but they're actually more predictable than you think, and in this book I'll teach you to figure them out. All of them. You'll learn how to push back on their power plays and when to stand up for yourself, even when you're scared (*especially* when you're scared). Look, when fear is running the show, you get totally wrapped up in your head. That's when you start missing all the most important cues that will help you with any dominating dude, power-hungry person, or childish antic you're dealing with.

I've been there. I've missed all the signals and then some. I didn't always have the backbone that I have today, the one that lets me run any room I'm in. Not even close. I once had a client who took me on a level-ten goose chase by acting like he was going to buy a very, very expensive home. I let this go on for years because I was too scared to call him on his lies. He was a fast-talking, good-looking, ultrarich (or so I thought) client who would use all these random facts and knowledge to try to outsmart me. I let my gut instincts about this guy being a total fraud get clouded by my doubt, and I ended up wasting hours and hours of my time on someone I knew was probably full of crap all along. There were so many red flags, like how I could find absolutely zero info about him, but he talked a huge game and tried to prove me wrong at every turn. He pulled out every stop to try to keep me from course-correcting the situation, like sending me screenshots of his bank summaries, showing the $362.9 million in his bank account as "proof of funds"—you can't make this shit up. They were obviously doctored, but I let him get to me. It took one too many situations where he was in the hospital "getting cancer treatment" right when the deal was supposed to go hard for me to start calling him on his shit. Listening to fear instead of myself resulted in so much of my time wasted, all my attention going to one single client and thus not building my pipeline of business, and more frustration than I could handle. If I had trusted myself a little more, I could have figured out the situation years earlier, before it totally blew up.

If you get thrown off course by big egos and intimidation, or if you get freaked out by high-stakes situations, it doesn't mean you're not competent or that you're doing something wrong. It just means you need a few reliable steps to demystify the actions of women like me, finding success through confidently controlling rooms in our own way. You'll find your own authentic way of taking control, too. This book is full of small changes you can make (and plenty of ridiculous stories from me) that will put you in control, not fear.

Once you start putting my advice into practice, you'll stop feeling "less than" the successful people around you. You won't be scared of those who try to kick you off your pedestal. (Because when you're a badass female, they'll try. Let's not forget that this world tells women every single day that they need to feel differently than they do. If you're killing it, they tell you that you're "too consumed by your job." If you're doubting, they tell you to get your shit together. You certainly aren't encouraged to be fearless by all the "change yourself" messages that you have to hear every single day.) Instead, you'll be able to use all the qualities that make you unique, and confidently bring them into each and every situation you're in. I'll let you in on all my secrets—from how I prepare for every single meeting (I mean Every. Single. One.) to the types of humor I think work best in every situation and how to try them and, most important, the personalities to look out for in every room and what to do with them.

Hopefully, this book will be a (gentle) kick in the butt to get your shit together and quit living with fear like it's your favorite handbag. It might live in your closet, because we all have fear, we all struggle with it, and fear is a normal thing, but it doesn't mean you need to take it with you to every crucial situation that you find yourself in. It doesn't go. What does is the most powerful version of yourself, every time. That's what you'll discover on the other side of implementing my strategies. Your most powerful, unencumbered-by-fear self.

FEAR IS JUST A FOUR-LETTER WORD

Chapter 1

....

KNOW
YOUR ROOM

A cigar bar and TVs. During a crucial development meeting, which is an early phase of planning a construction project that I'll eventually
list on the market, I could not get my client (the seller) off
the topic of a damn cigar bar and how each room needed
multiple televisions. I mean, are we opening a sports bar or
building a spec house? You get a guy in a room who likes to
build pretty things, and he wants to build the house for himself instead of building it for who the $70 million buyer
actually is. I know that buyer, and let me tell ya . . . they're
not looking for a damn cigar bar. This property was not
going to sell without architectural plans approved, which
is why I had worked my ass off to get all of the right people
into this meeting. I had to keep the team moving forward

if I wanted to ever get paid and avoid wasting the time of everyone there.

My cigar-obsessed client also happened to be a big producer in Hollywood. He had bought this huge piece of land in Malibu, all fourteen acres of it, in Serra Retreat, a gated premiere community in the heart of the area. He had bought it twenty-five years ago for significantly less, but home values had since shot through the roof. Some of the biggest sales lately had been in Malibu, so he saw dollar signs. They had already listed it once as a $23 million piece of dirt, and it wasn't selling. Honestly, it didn't look like it was going to ever get built by anyone—a seller or a buyer. This piece of land had a long history of litigation. Its topography was complicated. It was on a hillside. There had been several challenges with building on it—not unusual for Malibu. All of this was a turnoff to most buyers. There were no architectural plans attached, just a big, empty piece of land in Malibu that no one wanted to buy. If we could get the property listed with architectural plans submitted and approved by the Coastal Commission and then the city, it had a chance of selling at a much bigger number with RTI (ready-to-issue) permits. It was a long shot, but I had to get this client to wrap his head around going with a notable architect, which arguably would be expensive, and I had to get him focused on something he had just been sitting on for years. This piece of dirt was going to continue to just be a piece of dirt, unless I pushed the client to invest his money and time ASAP. The codes were going to change in Malibu and become even more restrictive than they already were. This was his last chance to take this land and turn it into something incredible.

Like his cigar-bar obsession, this guy was a total hoot. He was as fun as he was frenetic. Always in bright colors and golf attire (legit, lime green and canary yellow were among his favorite colors), he'd show up to the site excited to discuss progress and ideas. And maybe given that I was wearing red pumps to the same place, I shouldn't comment. Anyway, I really liked this guy—he was creative . . . inventive . . . smart. But he was about one more comment away from completely derailing our meeting and our ability to move this project forward.

So here I was with six people in my conference room trying to get on the same page about the architectural plans. I'd got both of the architects and their assistant. I had my client and his right-hand guy who managed the day-to-day. And I'd got an expediter from the city of Malibu to help walk us through this complicated process. There were millions on the line here for each of us.

When the architects presented their renderings of the property, explaining exactly how everything would be laid out, my client started asking highly specific questions . . . a lot of them. I was examining it from a bird's-eye view and thinking about space and light and integrity, and he was knee-deep in detail. This was one of our first meetings and he wanted to get into pizza-oven locations. He wanted that door to be two inches wider. At one point he got up from the table, speaking with his back to us while looking at the plans up close on the television. The architects had presented us with several options (five, to be exact), and they were hoping to narrow it down to two. But we were not getting anywhere because my client was now building his own home and moving into it next year with his wife and kids and having pizza night.

I knew this guy was a powerful personality and insanely creative. Anyone who googled his name could have figured that out based on how interesting and comedic his movies are. If I ignored that fact, we could have spent all day in the weeds, talking about details and never walking out of the meeting with the decisions needed in order to move forward. But because I knew exactly who was in the room, I had the answer about what to do next.

Here were my options at the time:

> *A)* I could piss off this star producer by getting annoyed, showing my agitation, and asserting that we needed to proceed my way in order to get it done.

B) I could follow his lead, get into the weeds of his on-spec choices, and lose my other teams (and my own sanity) entirely.

Obviously, neither of these would result in the outcome I wanted. So I needed to go with the next option, the correct one:

C) I had to find a way to make him feel heard, keep him focused, remind him that there's a reason I'm the expert on what sells, and channel his frenetic energy without offending him . . . so we could move forward.

Option C required a bit of finesse. I decided to get up and stand at the front of the room, so that I was standing *with* him; it put us on an equal physical playing field and commanded presence. I matched his excitement about how much possibility there was for this house—it's important for creatives (or anyone, for that matter, but creatives especially) to feel their ideas are being seen and appreciated—and then I asked whether his ultimate goal was to develop the property to sell for the highest possible price. He agreed. Sometimes you have to step back and remind everyone of the ultimate outcome. You'll make people feel like you're on their side, while managing to take back control of a conversation that's going off the rails. I explained to him that, as per our mutual goal, I had a better strategy for using his square footage. I gave him my two or three reasons why—all related to making him money, his biggest concern. Ultimately, I got him to incorporate a bar into the cigar room, so that it became a multi-functional space with the type of amenities that I know his target buyer is looking for today. Right there, I stopped his unproductive tangent. I reminded him why I was selling this property.

You could practically feel the collective sigh from everyone else in the room who needed this thing decided so we could go forward. It wasn't easy to navigate these personalities or this situation. But I got the outcome we needed, and it didn't require rocket science. It's not all god-given intuition, either. You can prepare for these difficult encounters by practicing my tried-and-true tactics. No matter who you have on your hands, though, you'll always get a meeting back on track by first making someone feel heard and then guiding them back to the bigger goal. Or you can ask them a clarifying question about what their objective is. It'll work every time.

FIGURE OUT WHO YOU'RE WITH

You likely spend a lot of time googling a date before you go out with them. It's such a simple thing. You can use Google to figure out where your date went to school and where they're working now (and if they've been arrested). Maybe you'll check Instagram and see if they're actually single. It's common sense. The FBI really should hire more women, because most of the girls in my office practically know their date's Social Security number before they go to dinner with them. We all do it, because it's worth doing the research when something important to you is on the line. I don't care if it's an interview, a big pitch, or a casual business meeting—more knowledge will always be more power.

You cannot expect to have the confidence to command a situation without fear, if you cannot make a genuine connection. That's where it all starts. If you know as much as humanly possibly about another individual, making a real connection becomes easier.

When I go into a meeting with someone new, I go deep. I find out everything, so that when I'm going into the room, I know where his head space might be and I have that background. So when he feeds me little hints during a meeting, I'm already correlating those to something I read or found out about him. Maybe his stock tanked, or maybe he's moving up in the world. If he got a promotion, I'll congratulate him. I'll look like I know who he is, what he does for a living, and what his needs are. That's very valuable.

If you don't take the time to go deep on the people you're meeting with, you not only miss the opportunity for connection but you risk getting caught off guard. Last year I got a call from a guy named Ron, who said he had a property for us to look at, and I agreed to meet him there. I had two pieces of information: his full name and the address of this property. That's it. Now, I could have walked in there blind, met this guy, asked a bunch of questions, and gone from there. But thank god I didn't.

When I googled him, I figured out all sorts of shit.

No. 1: He had a lending business and his broker's license.

No. 2: He had a few other developments.

No. 3: This property he was listing was owned by him and someone in his family.

Data point number one—that he was a broker not listing his own property—meant he was smart enough to know not to do this himself. This guy was clearly no idiot.

But it also meant that I needed to be ready to negotiate some sort of referral fee. Normally in this business, you fight for full commission. But data point number two told me that if he *did* ask me to negotiate my fee, I could ask him to give me business with his other developments.

I was right. He asked for a referral fee on this property he owned with his aunt, he promised me additional business, and we put together a really good listing because of it. There was a solid connection that has gone beyond this one listing, because I knew enough before that first meeting to create a situation that worked for both of us. Had I not gone deep on this guy, I would have potentially made a desperate choice in a moment of competitiveness to give him a referral fee and not ask for anything in return. I wouldn't have known my trade-offs. You never want to be put on the spot or blindsided—that's a major hit to take when all it would have required was ten minutes of stalking.

The internet can tell us a lot about the people we're working with and meeting. But not every important meeting is with someone you've never met before. On that Serra Retreat property in Malibu (the cigar guy), I had had *plenty* of meetings with all of these people before. But unless I had consciously taken the time to assess each person, why they were there, what their intended outcome was, and what made them tick, I probably wouldn't have taken the action that I did in that meeting that almost went left.

When you're doing your homework, here are a few items to consider that'll help you in the moment:

- *Their personality type:* You'll find out most of this in person (and I'll break down a few of the common ones I see and how to treat them later on in this chapter). But any particular strengths or weaknesses you can find out ahead of time will be useful. Knowing someone's personality type will help you make a more meaningful connection in the room. For example, if you know they're a dominant personality type, you can use questions to guide them to the area of conversation you'd like to arrive at, instead of talking over them, which will never work with a dominant personality. Or if they're passive, you'll need to speak up more and potentially even cheerlead them toward your common goal.

- *Their work:* What is their business? How long have they been doing it? What's happening in their career? Knowing someone's work will spotlight how their brain works day in and day out. For example, if they're in sales, you should be prepared that they're likely going to be challenging to negotiate with. Or if they're in marketing, you'll know the part of the process they'll care the most about (like images of the house, for example).

- ***Their passions:*** What are they actually passionate about? Are they involved in anything outside of work? You can use this information to establish common ground and have something to talk about that will put them at immediate ease.

- ***Their perspective:*** You can tell a lot about the lens someone sees the world through by paying attention to what they post on social media. You can often tell their views on core issues, and their view of themselves. For example, if they have many well-curated photos of themselves and clearly put a lot of effort into their social, you can tell they love being the center of attention, and you know to play to their ego. If there's a one-off grainy picture of their pet, they probably care less if you follow them or love their photos. You can use this info to your advantage by deciding whether to flatter and charm, or not. It'll help you better manage the room.

- *Their personal life:* Do they have kids? How many? Who are their friends? Are they single? You'll want to appeal to them from whatever place they're in—perhaps making comments about what you know of the kid's school, or about how hard dating can be these days. It establishes easy conversation.

Every nugget you can possibly get . . . get it. Whatever that is, it'll help you. Take the time to do the research on whoever is going to be in your room. Then take the time to memorize your research. I don't care if you have to freaking write it on your hand. Know it. That way, when you sit across from them, you'll better understand how to approach the situation coming at you and make a better connection.

PLEASE, LISTEN MORE

Most meetings don't go how I planned them. Some do, but rarely. Especially with people I've never met before. And while I could tell any of these people what makes me a badass and why someone should list their house with me over my competition, I don't do that initially. If I really want to win a deal or win over my clients, I go into meetings looking for the same few pieces of information. I've done the preparation that I outlined before, so I better understand who the person across from me is. Now I need to be in the moment, listening for where they're at.

I need to know:

1. *What are they into it for?* As in, how much have they spent on their home already? Sometimes I'll get stories of being ripped off, or contractors who went overboard, which tells me this person is looking to make up a deficit.

2. *How emotionally connected are they to what they're selling?* I don't ask this explicitly, of course, but I get to it by asking the history of the house. The answer is normally indicated by how much they talk about the time and effort that went into designing it, or some other emotional response about the memories they have made there.

I'm listening for this information. I'm also listening to what type of personality I have on my hands and if I need to watch out for it. I spend at least ten to fifteen minutes sussing out the situation, figuring out what kind of mood they're in, and getting them to deliver more and more information. Here are a few types of moods I'm paying attention for, because they affect how I go about the situation:

> *Agitated:* It's easy to tell someone when someone is having a difficult day if you're looking for the signs. Their energy seems strained, everything you say is problematic, they look down at their notes, and they don't seem to be really connecting. Note that it's easy to blame yourself for these foul moods, but nine times out of ten, invisible external factors are to blame. And if someone is downright angry (which is a more intense version of agitated), you can still use these tactics. When someone is in this type of mood, try not to focus on the difficult parts of the conversation. Punt those topics to a different day, and focus on things that are easy to decide on.

> *Excited:* When someone is in an overzealous or frenetic mood, I usually respond by matching their excitement. Otherwise, you might come across as overly guarded or judgmental. People tend to want to be in the same mood as those around them. Try to see whatever positivity

they're seeing, and they'll feel like you're totally on the same page.

Apathetic: That's a fucking mood. These people aren't invested in you or the project. So you have to work to get them to care, without coming across as desperate. It's a balancing act for sure. You have to continuously follow up and stay on top of them with communication and information, but you've got to keep it tight. It's the only way to shift them from not caring to giving a fuck, without making them feel like you're overwhelming. You can also look for connection elsewhere—as in, outside of the topic you're there to discuss. Finding commonality *anywhere* can be a major asset for dealing with apathetic people.

This is the type of information that you'll need to make a real connection and have an intelligent conversation.

Many times there's *more* than just one person in a room whom you need to understand in order to find the right path forward (and adjust your plan or your reactions accordingly). Recently I had a client looking for a house who's been one of my dearest friends since my early twenties. Cathy wanted a house with an open floor plan, new construction, and something modern. Oh, and she wanted it to *feel* good, too. She's clearly an emotional buyer. We looked at thirty-eight houses together. Ultimately, Cathy found a house that she felt like was the *one*, which was built by a developer.

In order for it to be hers, though, she needed to sell her home first, because she didn't want to carry two mortgages. Which meant we'd need a contingent offer: If we closed on hers, then we'd close on his within forty-eight hours. And this contingent offer would be in play for ninety days. But developers rarely take offers like this. They want to sell these houses as soon as they finish them. Every month they carry the home, it's more money out of their pocket.

So I did a lot of asking and a lot of listening with both of them. Once you find what both parties want—which sometimes requires serious digging—it's easier to find a creative, mutually agreeable solution. At the outset, it was possible we'd get a flat no. But it turned out that the inconvenience of waiting for Cathy's house to sell was worth it to him if Cathy just upped her offer by a modest amount—a price she was willing to pay. I mediated the conversation as best I could until we eventually had something we could all agree on. I had to know what each of them—my client and the seller—was in it for in order to make this a win for all of us.

In a negotiation, it's important to be thoughtful and consider every angle. You never want to be blindsided by something that you didn't ask about or information you didn't listen for. Never stop listening . . . not only for what they're saying but also, more important, for what they might *mean*. The questions you need to ask are going to be different depending on the situation, but the things you'll want to understand are all very similar. You want to get at what they want and why they want it.

Five Questions You Have to Get Answered

1. **What's their ideal outcome?** Ask things like "What's the best-case scenario for you here?" or "What would you like to accomplish by the time we finish here today?"

2. **How emotionally invested are they in that outcome?** Say things like "Tell me a bit about how you got here" or "Tell me more about why that's important to you."

3. **How did they arrive at the situation they're in?** Ask things like "What led you here?" or "Would anything have made it easier to get here today?"

4. **How can I help them achieve their goal?** Ask things like "Is there any area where you know

you need support?" or "Where do you think our paths could align the most?"

5. *What about my ideal outcome might be standing in their way?* Ask things like "What's the biggest hurdle you see us facing together?" or "Where could we meet on this?"

Remember, you don't have to ask anything explicitly. Rather, you're guiding the conversation to eventually get to these answers. It'll make it easier to find a win for everyone.

And a note about *where* you're allowing these meetings to happen: Any chance I have, I try to have meetings in *my* space. You have more control of the setup and energy when you do that. Plus, there are fewer variables that are new or unknown to you, which could screw up your situation. But look, I get it. I know not every important conversation or meeting or interview or pitch will happen in *your* space. You may not even have a space that's yours, which is completely fine and normal. Take them to your favorite lunch spot instead.

If you find yourself in someone else's space, position yourself so that you have as much of their focus as possible. People get so distracted by their in-boxes or get lost watching what is happening on their computer screens, and it can really break the momentum you might be building or distract you (or them) entirely. So if you can, get them away from their computer and on a walk. Or have them sit on the sofa instead. I do this all the time. If you can get their attention fully on you, then you're stacking your odds.

THE BIG PERSONALITIES CHEAT SHEET

Big personalities can be hard to manage, but if you want to gamble big, you'll have to learn how, because these are the personalities you'll come across. You can't let them scare or intimidate you. The way to manage them (and your own fear about them) is by knowing *who* they are. This goes beyond doing due diligence on them. I mean you have to understand what type of personality you're sitting with.

I know there are a million different personality types out there, but these are the types of influential personalities that I see every week—people with power, with money, with freedom, with privilege. You're bound to come across them in a high-level corporate environment, whether that's finance, sales, entertainment, creative, or something else entirely. If you understand who to look out for, it will help you in the long run. Here are four to keep an eye out for.

The Powerful Type

I have this one client, a crazy developer who's an absolute caricature of himself, and I secretly love him because he does not give two shits; he is doing him. He's dripping in diamonds. His watches and rings are encrusted with them. He has no less than six cars, and if there's a new Rolls out . . . he's got it. He's like a Kardashian sans the hair. And good luck keeping him focused! He's overzealous on just about everything. Needless to say, this guy is intense, so it's hard to hold it together when you're talking to him. So I speak slowly and with absolute conviction. Nothing can be wishy-washy, or I'll lose him. I always have a point of view, and he listens.

The thing about powerful types is that they let their ego drive them. He's always explaining things to you about the same topic that you're the expert on. He's got an "answer" (ahem, opinion) for everything. These people are used to being the most powerful person in the room, always, so they think they're an expert—and no fact will make them feel better or safer about what you have to say. I meet these people all the time in my business. They think they know how to price a house better than I do, and they're always telling me about the information they found (that actually has no relevance or context to it).

You have to let these guys think that they're in control.

If you're not sure with these people, they'll eat you alive. So always have 100 percent conviction about what you're saying. Don't say it if you're not certain—I've learned that the hard way. And if you don't have a clear answer, get back to them or say, "I need to check." When this happens to me, I try to get creative to find a way to make a meeting to circle back. In the meantime, I'll try to engage them on another facet, even if that's socially . . . versus losing them in that moment because I don't have the answer or because I'm not in that head space. Instead, I'll pause.

The Distracted One

This person has a really hard time sitting still. They're probably brilliant, but they have that nervous energy that spreads their focus all over the place. I call it *tick-tocking*, and you've probably seen it a million times. It's when the person you're meeting with or working with is in an entirely other head space. There's something else behind their eyes that they're thinking about even as they're talking to you. I'm always like, *Stop tick-tocking, dude.*

This is where less is more. You must think about your physical space a lot with these people. These are exactly the kinds of personalities that respond well to sitting on a couch and away from a computer. Minimize distractions and interruptions as much as possible. Ask a lot of questions. It'll force them to speak, which will keep their mind from wandering (and give you more information to work with). The questions you need to ask will be specific to the situation at hand, so when in doubt ask follow-ups using the old faithful: who, what, when, where, and why.

The Insane Creative

This personality type always leaves you feeling like you're about to get swept up into a total tornado. They're people just like my Hollywood producer client. They've got big ideas. They've got a million questions. They are living in their own movie and you are merely a costar. Many times they're brilliant. Many times they're hard to pin down.

The creative type is hard to keep focused, but they can also be very inspiring to you when you're sitting with them. Oftentimes their creativity will help you see outside the box and be really big-pictured instead. They'll get you thinking in a way you hadn't thought about before. While you'll likely learn something from them, you'll also have to work to home them in on the issue at hand, because they'll want to float above it. They don't prefer to be tactical, so you've got to be prepared for the blue-sky nature of this type of personality, which requires total preparation and constant redirection to the tactical needs at hand. But you can't make them feel slighted or their creativity unappreciated. You've got to remind them of the intended outcome and why you're the one to help get it there.

The True Collaborator

You want to be in a room with this person. They're the one who isn't completely driven by their ego. Team players are a best-case scenario because they don't think they're smarter than you (even though they're probably smart as hell). They know what they're doing but they're willing to work with you on it.

I'm in rooms with super powerful people all the time. But you don't know until you get this person talking for the first time that they're able to be warm, make jokes, and work to a common goal. You'll know you have a team player on your hands because they'll ask you questions, they'll enlist your opinion, and everything will feel more like a discussion and less like a battle.

Build rapport with these people. Work with them time and time again when you spot them.

Remember, none of these powerful personality types are bad necessarily. In the case of the first three, they're just some of the most difficult to navigate when they're in the room with you and are standing between you and the outcome that you want. Assessing if you're about to be in the room with one of them (or what to look out for when you go into any room with a new person) is part of the home-work you need to do to not get swept up in fear when you meet them. Now you know what to look for.

IT'S OKAY TO BE A CHAMELEON

Most performers know that every audience is going to be different. Back in the day, in my singing group, Everything Nice—yes, I was the rapper, and we were chasing our dream of being the next Spice Girls—one performance would be so good I'd plan to quit school and work on my Grammy acceptance speech . . . and then the next night we'd bomb so badly that I would have to apologize to my dad and tell him I would still be attending USC one day. Every crowd was a toss-up.

When we were performing, we'd always make adjustments to the performance depending on the audience that was listening. In business, and in my life, I still get to read the room and adjust which part of myself I want to be. If I figure out that someone's in a shitty mood and needs to air their opinions, I'll let them get all of that off their chest. I'll be my most understanding and empathetic self and genuinely listen to what they're going through. I never steamroll someone needing a moment.

This is why knowing who's in the room with you is so important. Once you have the information of who's across from you and what's motivating them, you can adjust your approach accordingly. You've got to be a chameleon sometimes and be willing to change your colors. Chameleons don't wake up and decide it'd be better to be a polar bear that day. They're always themselves, just with a little different coloring from one situation to the next. If you're going to be successful, you've got to be the same.

You can't go confidently into every room the exact same way. Just today I had back-to-back meetings that each required something different of me. First I met with a buyer who's based in New York City on the Upper East Side. I wore no-nonsense black slacks and top with understated accessories and talked about the building with her. To win her over, I focused heavily on the understated nature of the architecture and the high quality of the finishes, and slid some fashion into the conversation. Then I had a meeting with a female exec at E! Entertainment. I was able to really be myself (a little sarcastic, a hint of self-deprecation, and the proper amount of boss). Then I headed to Pasadena, where I met with a seller whose dad just passed away, which required switching gears to be a little more sensitive about what he was going through. But I also showed him that I'm a tough negotiator who will protect his asset at any cost. Finally, I ended my day dropping all of that authoritative nature to talk and connect with my teenage daughter. She's just turned fourteen, and we know what that can be like. So, in order to connect, I really had to take the judgmental mom hat off and relate.

I'm still Tracy in every single one of these rooms. Like a chameleon, I don't become anyone else. If you go too far in any direction, becoming something that you're not, you lose your effectiveness and your ability to be convincing. People can tell from a mile away when you're being inauthentic or you're trying to say whatever you think they want to hear. It won't work.

The point of knowing the audience and becoming a chameleon isn't so that you can give them the colors you *think* they want to see. It's so that you can bring the best version of yourself that you *think* will help you be successful. It will give you the confidence to handle any situation that might scare you. We're not trying to lose you in the process. You've seen the friend or the colleague who fucks this up in social situations all the time. She'll be talking to you over lunch about how she can't stand something, maybe a movie everyone's buzzing about. Then, the next day in a wider group of people talking about the same movie, she all of sudden has a change of heart and chimes in about how much she loves it. You're over there listening like *WTF?* That's a person who's willing to become someone

she's not for the sake of being liked or fitting into the conversation. That's not a person who has a backbone.

I've made this mistake before. I've wanted to win someone over so badly that I kept trying to do whatever it took
to get them on my side. I'm not the type of woman who
takes any shit, but even the best of us are going to mess this
up here and there. And because of my eagerness to own the
room, I ignored so many indicators that I was getting away
from my true self (and friends and family telling me to
separate from this situation). It didn't matter how many
times I tried to fit what this client wanted; I wasn't going to
come out on top of this one. And I risked losing myself in
the process.

The goal is to stay true to yourself but be flexible in
what parts of yourself that you're bringing to each situation. For example, I always go above and beyond for my
clients. That's what I do. But I'm also tough in knowing
what I deserve. In the past, I have cut my commission or
offered to oversee the staging of someone's house (which
is *not* what I do) or sat at the first open house or worked
super late on a night I was supposed to be with my daughters for clients who have respect for me and what I bring to
the table. Humor and integrity are two qualities about myself I never negotiate on. If someone expects me to not make
a joke, or to do something shady, I absolutely won't be a
part of the situation. I can flex on my "toughness," but not

on my humor or integrity. If something makes you feel like you're less of yourself, then you can't do it. You can have more confidence holding your ground, and figuring out where *you* feel comfortable flexing and where you don't, because now you understand how to do that based on who exactly is in your room. Then adjust yourself accordingly. So remember, to command the room you're going to have to **know your room.**

Knowing your room demands:

- *Preparing.* Do your homework. Know who they are *before* you're in the room so that you can make the best possible connection.
- *Assessing* whether there are any powerful personality types and reminding yourself how to handle them.
- *Listening* for key information that helps you understand the motivations of the people you're engaging with.

And then you get to change your colors accordingly. Your goal is always to garner people's trust and attention. Knowing who that person is goes beyond their bio, and it allows you to adjust who you are in that room at that moment. The truth is, people are making a decision that's both factual and emotional. They won't trust your input or follow your lead if they're not emotionally invested. If they feel a trust and confidence in you, you've already won. You'll feel confident in yourself when you know exactly who you're dealing with. Eventually, you'll have made a real connection that both people value. Then you can lead the room, and the people in it, to exactly where you want.

....

QUIT HIDING YOUR YOUR INTUITION

....

QUIT HIDING YOUR INTUITION

W hen a potential buyer tells me, "This house is going to be mine," it's normally a good thing. Especially when that house is $75 million. But I had a weird feeling about this very fast-talking, sarcastic buyer—we'll call him Ted (sounds sleazy enough, doesn't it? Sorry if you have a Ted you know and love). Ted was looking at my client's property in Malibu. So I did what I often do when my instincts are trying to tell me something: I didn't say much and chose to just listen to him as we drove. I was becoming increasingly concerned that this person was not who he said he was. Or that something else was off. I couldn't totally put my finger on it, but I had a feeling this wasn't going to be a straightforward and exciting real estate deal.

You can imagine my excitement when Ted invited me

and Erika from my team to dinner on a Tuesday night. I wanted to be at home with my two daughters, but this was too big a possible deal to ignore. Plus, I figured that if I was right about Ted, I'd probably know from stopping by dinner. So we got there, and this guy had painted a pretty good scene—I'll give him that. He had a dinner table full of rich old men in fancy suits, all fairly conservative. Either he was setting up the dinner to look more credible, or this was genuine. I sat through dinner and still couldn't get a read. But I needed to, because if I invited him as a next step to meet my client, the seller of this massive property, who was also a live-wire personality, and it went poorly because he was a fraud or whatever, my whole portfolio would be on the line. But if it went well, it could mean a huge deal and millions of dollars in commission for me and my team.

Ultimately, I decided to set up a dinner a few nights later between Ted, my client, and me. I seated myself (purposely) between them. The dinner meeting started, and Ted began talking over everyone at the table. He was being incredibly sarcastic, and I was getting increasingly uneasy. I tried to direct the conversation toward the real estate deal at hand, and my client (a lunatic himself) said, "What? Are we moving too quickly for you, Trace?" Then Ted piled on by refusing to shut up about investment deals and kickbacks and everything *but a real estate transaction.* Essentially he used me to get in front of my high-net-worth client so he could propose investment options in my client's portfolio of developments and free up money while getting a better deal on the house he said "had to be his." I fucking knew it.

Oh but wait, it gets worse. When I pointed out that I don't get paid in a deal like this—because it's not a real estate transaction—Ted suggested a "finder's fee." As I began to explain why I'd need to talk to my lawyer about that, he cut me off. To which I interrupted him to say, "Would you like to let me finish?"

"You're awfully feisty tonight. What, is it that time of the month?"

Yup. Honey, he said it. Here I am sitting dead center between two egomaniacs, with twenty years of experience under my belt, and I'm still having my period being held against me while standing up for my business and for myself. It's incensing, and I know we've all been there. I had three options here:

A) Fumble my response and awkwardly change the subject.

B) Lash out with "No, I'm not on my fucking period, thanks" and get visibly uncomfortable, moving around in my chair, eyes darting across the room, and about to cry.

C) Confront it head on and say, "We're in a business meeting, and I'd like us to be as professional
as possible and focus on the real estate. When
you're ready to apologize, you let me know and
I'll rejoin this conversation."

Obviously, C would have been the right choice. But I
went with route B—because I had gotten so far away from
my own instincts and let theirs run the show instead. I felt
completely humiliated, and these guys were talking down
to me like I was some idiot. I should've known not to
second-guess myself when my intuition told me to speak
up about something totally inappropriate. This is one of
the situations where your intuition is most trustworthy:
when you want to call someone out. Just fucking do it.
Although you'll notice I went about it in a specific way.
We'll get to that in a second.

Intuition can be used everywhere. Or rather, it should
be. You're not making the best decisions possible if you're
not using your intuition in every scenario. It guides everything for me, as it should. Plus, I think women have better
intuition than men.

Intuition is not "seeing things." I've got girlfriends in LA
who tell me, "I think I'm psychic." *Are you? Or are you just
having a really connected experience?* Intuition doesn't mean
you're a witch. There's nothing woo-woo about it. It's sim-

ply tuning in to what's not being said and feeling all the pieces of a situation come together, instead of taking only what's in front of you as fact. Everybody has this ability to use their intuition to see the problem at hand and get clues on how to solve it. It requires being very aware of everything that's happening around you—your own feelings, your own experience, the people in front of you, what's being said, and (sometimes just as important) what's not being said.

I use my intuition to determine when I should call it like it is. Sometimes we've got to go for it and put ourselves in the arena. We're all kind of scared. Maybe I'll get turned down, but if I feel my time is right, my intuition helps tell me when to act on it.

In this chapter, I'll teach you how to listen to your intuition. And I'll give you scripts for channeling your intuition into calm, cool, collected words that'll help you get the best possible outcome.

CALLING IT LIKE IT IS

With Ted, I completely lost my ability to have a (trained) knee-jerk reaction—which I'm normally so good at. Ultimately, I ended up excusing myself to go to the restroom so I could compose myself, because I was on the verge of tears and wanted to get the fuck out of there. I was pissed that I'd ignored my gut feeling about this guy and pissed I had lost control of the meeting. (Isn't it insane how they're the ones saying shit like that and we're mad at *ourselves*?) I was mad, so mad when I left that dinner, mainly because I'd ignored my instincts and gotten thrown off my game in the face of two big personalities and their rude comments. It happens to all of us. Even the super successful, super experienced.

It would have been so much nicer if I could have just taken control of that situation (and any, for that matter) while just relaxing. Think about it—you could chill out, sip your rosé, and never have to get the least bit uncomfortable. You'd never have to sit at a dinner where people go on a power trip and make you feel like crap while they do. That would make this whole success thing so much easier. You wouldn't have to worry about pleasing people, or fitting in, or calling people out when you've been undermined. Reality is a bit different. As it turns out, you've got to show up front and center, where there's simply no hiding.

It might be scary at first, and you might get it wrong sometimes. If you're in an interview and you totally shut down when someone says something totally inappropriate . . . I get it. If someone takes your idea and acts like it's theirs . . . and you feel so angry that you don't trust yourself to say anything at all . . . I also get it. If you find out that someone has said something negative and untrue about you in order to burn your reputation, you better believe that I get that, too. In any of these situations where you're slighted, pushed around, intimidated, feeling off or feeling something, your intuition about what to do next requires some trial and error. I'd like you to learn from my trials, though, so you have fewer error-earned lessons.

A (TRAINED) KNEE-JERK REACTION

People always say, "Don't be reactive." But why the fuck not? You can react without being reactionary. You can be emotional and strategic at the same time. The trick is to not lead with emotion in your response. Fuel your strength, your opinion, and your response with your emotion. Just don't let it steer the ship.

In the moments when you need to showcase power, less is more. You can make a statement in as little as one sentence or one move of your body or one direct, piercing look. A very good, very focused knee-jerk reaction incorporates a few of these:

> *Fewer words.* Make your statement as direct and
> pointed as possible. It may take you a minute to

gather your thoughts; that's fine. Silence is deafening to people.

Less shifty eyes. Hold direct and unflinching eye contact.

Less movement in your chair. Hold your body still and in control.

As I mentioned, I did the opposite of all of this with Ted when he asked if I was on my period. I was shifty, shaky, and verbal. If I had taken a few beats, gathered myself, and focused my body, I could have said (easily), "If you speak to me like that again, this meeting is going to be over." That one sentence followed by silence, direct eye contact, and steadiness would have made him incredibly uncomfortable. And I would have regained control of the dinner.

When confronting inappropriate behavior, I try to:

- Be calm but direct
- Cite the business context and say I want to focus on that
- Ask for an apology or set a boundary ("This meeting will be over if you speak to me like that again")

(Now, this is probably a great time to mention that sexual harassment in the workplace is never okay and is against the law. If that's what you're experiencing, consult your workplace policies and HR department.)

If you're like many people I know, you're planning twenty-seven steps down the road before you follow your gut. You're thinking about all the worst ways that a situation can blow back or blow up based on something that you do today. You can't live like that. If you're constantly worried about what could hurt you, that mentality will keep you hiding forever. That unleashes a dragon of worst-case scenarios, most of which aren't remotely realistic. The only way to ever be heard is by throwing your fear aside and just doing it. Saying it. Taking the step rather than living in fear.

If you try to cheat me, undercut my success, or go around me, that's worth putting my boxing gloves on for. I'll go wherever intuition takes me. I take those things *very* personally, and I'm coming after anyone who tries them. If anyone tells you that you shouldn't, I'm telling you that you sure as fuck should. It's not even about getting the job or the promotion or the deal. It's bigger than that. On principle, you shouldn't let someone purposely bring you down to further their own career. If you don't speak up or you table a confrontation for later because you don't want to stir the pot, then you're being ineffective and not embracing your full power. Period. Does it require growth to get to that place where you confront people for overlooking you for something? Yes. But once you get there, it is incredibly liberating to have no problem looking someone in the eye and saying, "I see what you're doing and it's not working. I will not be challenged."

I've said that line plenty of times, but none more emphatically than when I was brought on as the sales director for a luxury development in LA. Some of the sales team was resentful about my role, because I didn't sit in the sales gallery full time (I have a team and a business of my own). However, the leadership team wasn't paying me to be a butt in a seat; they were putting me in this role to be a voice for this project, hold deals together when they were falling apart, and bring in brokers I had personal relationships with.

I quickly went from feeling *honored* to be in this position to it being a huge interpersonal struggle within the team. Where I think it went south was that the sales team in place felt like they had been slighted because they sat there every day, and if anyone was going to be named sales director, they believed it should have been one of them and not me. In their eyes, I wasn't in that office daily and rather was taking care of my own business. While all of the leadership had agreed on this setup, it created an enormous amount of tension. Every time I would try to do my job, which I had been specifically asked to do, I would get blocked in house by an agent who felt like I'd stolen their spot. It was not pretty. At every turn I felt like someone was attempting to go around me.

So it really didn't surprise me when Jacob did. He was one of the guys who thought he should be sales director instead of me. He and I were working on a multimillion-dollar deal to sell a big unit to a buyer, and they wanted to submit an offer. Then I got texts from the buyer's broker saying he had just been asked to submit his client's offer directly to Jacob. And to Jacob only. The broker thought it was strange that he'd been specifically directed to send it *only* to Jacob, even though I was a broker on this deal, too. Not something you should be doing to your sales director. Not to mention I had a personal relationship with the family of the buyer.

So I picked up the phone and called Jacob directly. "Is there a reason you asked for the offer to be submitted only to you?" And he, of course, started nervously denying it. I didn't back down. "So then can you explain why I've got texts from the other broker saying he thinks it's weird that you specifically asked for this offer to only be sent to you?" To which he started babbling about this being "standard" procedure. He complained that I "always did this" when he was just following protocol. I didn't back down and said,

"Always do what?" He tried to tell me to calm down and that I was overreacting. And I continued, saying, "Number one, don't tell me to calm down. I'm calm AF. Number two, don't ever try to cut me out of *our* deal again. The only reason you didn't put me on that deal is to undermine my seniority and make it look like it came to you directly so you could forward it on to ownership."

I was both professional and calm. I didn't raise my voice, but I was serious. He was trying to make me look like I didn't care and wasn't involved. He wanted to be the guy who closed this deal. He was holding on to whatever corporate power he felt like he was owed for having the position he had. This was a guy who would throw people under a bus to make sure he was advancing. I saw right through his bullshit. And I wasn't staying quiet about any action that undermines my role anymore. If I didn't say anything, it would all remain the same.

In this situation, I sent the following email to Jacob and CCed our leadership, because it's always important to put things in writing.

From: Tracy Tutor
Date: Monday, July 1, 2019 at 2:06:18 PM
Subject: Re: showing
To: Jacob
Cc: Leadership

Jacob,

Moving forward, do not ask the agents we work with to only send the offer to you. Greg (Donna's agent) reached out to me directly and said he just submitted the offer and was asked to only send it to you. He thought that was strange because he knows I have represented different members of the family and should be involved. I shouldn't have to hear from him rather than my own team about the offer, therefore undermining our team. I am the Sales Director (which I seem to keep having to remind you) and will not have you undermining me.

Forward the offer to me for review and I will forward to the team, making it abundantly clear that you are on the deal. That seems to be your concern. If I am wrong, let me know. But please don't go around me again.

Tracy

If you've got a "Jacob" in your life, you've got to be ready to listen to what you're feeling about the situation and box him out. Remember, to make your knee-jerk reaction trained and effective, be calm and direct.

A CONFRONTATION BLUEPRINT

You can use these steps to call out someone on their crap on behalf of someone you care about—like a team member, family, or friend. If you feel like you need to fight someone, or on behalf of someone, confrontation is a great tool that you can use to win.

What to Do

1. ***Lead with a question.*** I like giving someone the opportunity to explain, which is why I always lead with a question. Sometimes it will have a tone of sarcasm, like "Am I crazy, or did you just go around me on purpose?" Other questions that work to ultimately get them to tell you what you already know:

   - Is there anything you want to tell me?
   - Am I wrong or have I lost my mind?
   - Is there something you want to share?
   - Would you rather I hear this from you or from someone else?

   You want to drive the point home with these questions. Reactions will often be defensive, which tells you right off the bat that they knew *exactly* what they were doing. You're not mistaken or crazy or overreacting; you're experiencing this exactly as it is.

2. ***Give space to explain.*** It's important to go back through your understanding and perception of what happened (or even your gut instinct about what went down). You really throw someone off balance when you speak with the confidence that you already know what they did. Giving space allows them the opportunity to bury themselves, which they'll likely do when they've wronged you. I typically will say, "Tell me if I'm wrong . . ." or "Let me know if this is off . . ." and I say it in a tone of voice that is not messing around. If you weren't copied on an email, for example, maybe it's an oversight or maybe it's one person trying to make themselves look good.

3. ***End the conversation.*** If you find yourself going in circles with someone, and they refuse to be accountable for their actions, you'll catch them off guard by shutting the conversation down. Fighting with silence is a powerful way to get

your point across. Or if you're dealing with someone who also knows how to fight, you can conclude a callout by wrapping it up and declaring as much. "Conversation's over." You literally say that. Or "I'm not going to have this conversation with you. We can discuss this another time. Right now, I'm done with it." Or "We've talked enough. I'll follow up in writing." There's obviously potential for backlash, but it's worth it when you're speaking your truth. When you do, you'll notice how powerful you feel, and you'll be more inclined to do it again. You'll notice that even when there is backlash, you'll survive it. That gives you more confidence to do it in the future.

4. *Follow up in email.* I'm always much more careful about what I put in writing than about what I say on the phone. Regardless, every callout needs to be recapped in writing so you have it.

5. *Move on.* You've got to move on and act professional the next time you see each other. The incident doesn't have to be rehashed unless someone else brings it up or it happens again.

DON'T SECOND-GUESS YOURSELF

I'm completely willing to sacrifice carefully crafted eloquence for speaking my mind in the moment. That's exactly what I did when I saw that a major real estate publication, *The Real Deal*—which is both online and in print in New York and LA—was putting on a large event and had invited ten LA-based brokers to speak on panels. I had received an invitation from a sponsor to attend the conference as their guest. I was shooting for *Million Dollar Listing Los Angeles* and was on a five-minute break, so I opened up the website to take a look at what they were doing, and I realized that 90 percent of their panelists were white males; there was just one female. I had a problem with that because over 60 percent of the real estate community across the nation is female, and we should have been represented. Maybe it was the mood I was in, but it really pissed me off. So I immediately responded to the email invite and said I couldn't attend this event because I found it offensive. I was so annoyed by the whole thing that I decided to do an Instagram story. I didn't ask anyone's opinion; I just did it.

And I held nothing back. I told my followers what I had seen—the lack of diversity on their panels—and asked my community to step up and boycott them until they could figure it out and get it right. I also specifically directed a request to my friends Josh Altman and Josh Flagg, costars on my show and panelists at the event, to put their foot down and do the right thing—otherwise nothing was going to change. It was all about advertising dollars to *The Real Deal*, but they needed to be held responsible. I told everyone I wanted honest accountability, not some glossy PR political statement. Eventually *The Real Deal* issued an apology. They wrote:

> *Dear @tracytutor, thank you. It's not easy to digest what you said, but when you're right, you're right. We can and should do better.*
>
> *For over sixteen years, we've prided ourselves on being the publication that pulls no punches, that holds the industry accountable for everything from misleading marketing tactics, to the massive gender disparity in the C-suite, to sexual harassment. We were among the first outlets to do a deep dive into real estate's reckoning with the #MeToo movement and we were the first outlet to crunch the numbers on how stark the gender gap is. We've done these stories despite facing immense pressure, both legal and financial, from industry figures, including some of our biggest advertisers.*
>
> *Our events strive to further this mandate. We aim to present a discussion that is reflective of the demograph-*

ics of the industry we cover. Our previous panels, all over the country and the world, have showcased the views of a broad array of leading industry professionals, female and male, white and black, gay and straight. This time, we fell short. We're going to take a hard look at how we put our panels together so that this doesn't happen again.

We also want to hear from our readers and followers. Rather than leave things in the dark, talk to us: Tell us what you'd like to see improve. For starters, we saw that @thejoshaltman is giving up his spot on the panel. We'd love you, our readers, to nominate a top female real estate professional from the L.A. area that you believe deserves to take his place in addition to the two female powerhouses we currently have as part of the panel discussions. Tag your nominee below or email us at megan@therealdeal.com.

Sincerely @mrkorangy, Publisher

Not only did they acknowledge my callout, but Josh Altman, Ron Smith, and Josh Flagg all stepped down from the panel within a few days of my post. For me, it wasn't about some grand statement. I wasn't trying to start a war. It was a battle that was local to me that I knew I should win. I had something important to say, and I came forward with it. I didn't want to get into a tit-for-tat or a back-and-forth with a big media publication. This was authentic to me and unfiltered on social media. If I'd started crafting different responses, my point would have lost its effectiveness. Listen, I'm not a fucking trailblazer, and I'm not trying to be. More, ignoring women in the industry straight bugged the hell out of me. It's just that simple. It was a passionate but deliberate response. It was backed by data, fueled by emotion, specific to me, and finished with a request.

Seven years ago, maybe I would have sat on this very reaction. I probably would have talked to my team, called a colleague, gotten a take from everyone involved, and potentially lost the nerve to say anything bold. The result would have been a watered-down version of what my instincts were. Sure I could have slept on it, only to wake up the next day and see that both the moment and my reaction were lost.

You lose your effectiveness if you don't trust your own instincts. Not trusting your gut shows up in a few ways:

- Asking for everyone else's take on the situation
- Asking other people what you should do
- Sleeping on it or delaying action
- Staying quiet and saying nothing at all
- Qualifying everything you say ("I might be wrong here, but . . .")

BLOWBACK IS REAL. YOU'LL DEAL.

Maybe there's a time when I'll regret saying something. But not yet. I think that's because if it's your *truth* and honest to you, there's not much to regret. That doesn't mean people won't try to make you regret it—which is a tactic used to keep you from speaking up. I've had plenty of blowback, but when you know it was your true reaction, it's easier to stand by what you said and did.

There's a learning curve to following your intuition, for sure. You'll screw this up by overreacting or not reacting at all, even though your intuition is always there. We all get gut feelings; we just have to learn the tactics that help us train our knee-jerk reaction to what we're feeling in the moment. You may be too direct and offensive the first time you try to go with your feeling in the moment. Or you may only see your one point of view and miss the whole picture entirely. That's when you'll face blowback.

When I stood up to *The Real Deal* by speaking up, they used what I said to challenge Bravo for not being inclusive. I heard from people in attendance at the actual panel that the moderator said something along the lines of questioning Bravo about *their* inclusivity and representation. Which makes no sense because the network as a whole has always been way ahead of the curve in giving the spotlight to everyone regardless of race, sexual preference, age, or gender. They're actually *known* for it. Because I used my voice, they flipped the script onto Bravo, which could potentially cause backlash for me. I don't yet know if this will come back, but I can't let worrying about that affect what I do today. I've spent too many years in that head space, and it got me nowhere but more worked up, anxious, and scared. I can't hide because of those worries anymore. Trust me, hiding is never worth it.

Look, if you're doing what's best for you and saying what's true to you, you might piss some people off. They'll recover, and if they don't . . . clip 'em out of your life, because you only have this one life to live. Don't waste it making choices that are wrapped up in someone else's shit. Dig deep and do you, or else you'll spend your entire life dependent on the validation that you may or may not get from someone else. At a certain point, you have to put out there what you're going to put out. However, people are going to view it how they're going to view it. Tell yourself what I'm often repeating in my head: *I am who I am.*

You are who you are. If you choose to hide that, you're missing out on so much.

SHARPENING THE BLADE

Your intuition can do more than tell you when to speak up, of course. It can help you everywhere. Here's how I use intuition to inform my life:

When to get out of the room: Do I need to leave the date? Do I need to back out of this business deal because it's all about to implode? If I feel what's really going on, I can answer this and move accordingly.

When to push the envelope: If I'm paying attention to my intuition, I'll know when I can ask for more on my commission. I'll also know when it's the right situation to negotiate down. Intuition will give you a really clear sense of boundaries and how far you can take something.

When to take a big risk: I always know when to put myself out there and what risk will likely be worth it, using my intuition when the facts say something else. Sometimes we've got to go for it and put ourselves in the arena. We're all kind of scared. Sometimes the risk pays off and sometimes it doesn't. Maybe I'll get turned down, but I felt my time was right, and my intuition helps tell me when to act on it. Whether it's looking for a new job, negotiating for the first time, moving across the country, investing in yourself, hiring someone for your business, or doing your first speaking engagement, big risks are always personal. What feels risky to you may feel different for someone else.

When to ask more questions: Often, before doing any of the above, I'll sense that the best thing to do is ask clarifying questions. I'll ask if I heard them right and repeat what they said. I'll ask for specific information that might be a bit ballsy.

It takes practice to hear your intuition, though. That's what this section is about. Here are some small but important ways to begin owning your truth, start tuning in to your intuition about a situation, and see how it guides your response (trained knee-jerk reactions included):

- Talk to friends about something that you heard on a podcast that you didn't agree with, and see how it feels. This approach isn't personal to

anyone and lets you test what it feels like to disagree.

- Say no to something and hold a boundary that
may not please the other person asking for your
time.
- Speak up when someone is gossiping. Tell them
that you'd prefer to not talk about people who
aren't in the room.
- Share an opposing point or opinion in a meeting
with peers.

As you're working toward accessing all the parts of
yourself and *showing* them, you've got to surround yourself with people who don't expect you to hide. Especially
as you get more and more bold. There will be some people
in your life who, for whatever reason, would rather that
you stayed small. (Trust me, I've been there. I've had people super close to me not want me to *do me*.) It's usually
always selfish. It's always about them. Remember that. If
you're not sure who those supportive people are, ask
yourself:

- Who am I most comfortable around or the most
at ease being myself with?
- Who helps me see the things that are funny, interesting, or unique about myself?

- Which friends have the most "you do you" vibes?

Friends have called me "an acquired taste." While I'd like to believe that they're talking about a taste for sophistication, humor, and warmth, I'm not so sure that's what they mean—ha! But I see their point. Because from the earliest time I can remember, I've been relentless about sharing what's on my mind. Since I was a kid, I've always been standing up to the bullies. I would see other girls who were making certain people feel bad, and I would go crazy. I got a reputation for being a bitch because I'd verbally annihilate anyone taking advantage of weaker personalities. I couldn't hide my feelings that people shouldn't be treated like that, and I let it be known.

Being you, doing you, saying you, embracing you . . . It's easier when you spend your days with people who don't ask you to hide. I joke that I like to keep myself in the gay bubble—hanging with fabulous gay men who always tell me I'm awesome and don't try to sleep with me. In reality, the "gay bubble" is a love bubble, a soft place to land with people who always let me be myself. My best girlfriends do the same for me. They are my true north. You don't need everyone to be 100 percent on your team, because they won't be. But you do want to make sure that your inner circle is full of people who are pulling you out into the sunshine instead of pushing you into the shadows.

DON'T HIDE YOUR INTUITION . . . BUT DO COMPARTMENTALIZE YOUR EMOTIONS

You can't have diarrhea of the mouth all over your professional life. You have to learn how to put that stuff away. Just because you shouldn't hide what's on your mind doesn't mean you need to say *everything*. There's a major difference between sharing your instincts, your truth, and your thoughts—and sharing every detail of your life.

No emotion is ever totally unproductive—anger, jealousy, envy, sadness, whatever it is, you've got to feel it to be human and have compassion for other people. When some emotions become straight unproductive is when they're in excess and when your reaction to one event—say, a fight with a loved one—starts affecting your reaction to other events—like an offhand remark someone made in the middle of a deal negotiation—leading you to overreact or misinterpret. I remember when I was going through my divorce, I'd have a terrible day dealing with attorneys, and then I'd have to turn around and be firing on all cylinders to negotiate a dying deal. I learned to channel that frustrating energy into productive energy by throwing myself into the project at hand with extra intensity. Total focus feels good. Getting results feels even better. That's the helpful thing about compartmentalizing—you can put away the details, but you can redirect your negative emotions to fuel the situation for your benefit. Maybe you're down or heartbroken or feeling a little depressed—put away that piece, the cause, but keep the effect.

Part of compartmentalizing is knowing what to say when. You're not going to say everything on your mind at all times to everyone. Later you're going to learn exactly how to read your audience and when to use what parts of yourself. But what's important from the start is to move fear out of the driver's seat. It's keeping you from accessing all the bold and direct parts of you that you'll so badly need going forward. If you can start to see where you're playing small, playing it safe, and playing to please, you can start to change it. Soon you'll quit hiding for good and move to the front and center of your own life.

You're going to experience overt power plays that will piss you off. They might even make you rage. You have a choice to be scared of what you're feeling or to learn how to listen to your gut . . . and even more so, do something about what you're hearing. You intuition may take you to some unknown places—places that require you to call people out, to speak up, to disagree, or to call attention to yourself—trust me that you can handle it. If you'll let your intuition be seen (by yourself), you allow yourself to be seen by the world.

Chapter 3

....

FIGHT LIKE
A GIRL

We're made to feel small in a host of sly, underhanded ways that add up like paper cuts: after a while, they start to really hurt. You'll need to fight back in ways that are quiet yet powerful. Not every situation worth fighting for will be completely obvious to others. You don't have to be royally screwed over in order to take up a battle. You're allowed to take things personally. Sometimes the most important issues that you'll step in the ring for are the subtler power moves people use against you. While the last chapter taught you to speak your truth when you've been wronged or when you have a strong point of view, this chapter will teach you to counter subtle power moves with some of your own.

And for the love of god, we've got to stop thinking about fighting as a bad thing. You can't avoid it, and why should you? The men you're fighting are way less powerful than you think. I always come back to this quote by Michelle Obama when I'm feeling intimidated: "I have been at probably every powerful table that you can think of, I have worked at nonprofits, I have been at foundations, I have worked in corporations, served on corporate boards, I have been at G-summits, I have sat in at the U.N.: They are not that smart." I find that men especially know we're intuitive and have great instincts, and deep down I think it scares them, especially when we enter any disagreement or confrontation. We all know that women have been outsmarting men since the beginning of time, even if most times they can physically dominate us. But we have something they don't. Our intuition and empathy can be strengths that no one (particularly men) sees coming, especially given how easily manipulated they are if you know their weaknesses. They can be used to fight, which is why fighting isn't something you need to shy away from.

The battlegrounds you'll find yourself on can seem rather unassuming from the outside. But you'll know because you'll feel someone trying to steal the internal power you've tapped into. This shows up when people don't take you seriously about your goals or act surprised you'd apply for a promotion. Or when people are playing a zero-sum game, and they feel like your success at an organization threatens theirs. You'll also notice these battleground moments in friendships, when you're getting false enthusiasm for something great that just happened to you, instead of sincere encouragement. These are all the small ways people try to make small cuts at us, hoping to intimidate us into playing small so they can feel better about themselves.

I don't have any space in my life for being pushed around without saying something about it. I'm a pro at dealing with assholes; it's basically my daily life. Here's what to watch out for, which are often sure signs someone is trying to intimidate you:

- They cut you off.
- They ask you a question and then don't give you the chance to answer.
- They start a conversation with "I'm not happy," which immediately puts you on the defensive or in the wrong.
- They raise their voice.
- They stand over you.
- They send an onslaught of calls or texts.
- They schedule a meeting without giving you any idea or context regarding what it's about.
- They leave you in the dark, keeping you out of conversations you should be in.

- They add to a meeting a bunch of people from their side whom you have no relationship with— like an attorney, other team members, etc.
- They talk to other people about your relationship.
- They say nothing.
- They begin an important meeting or conversation with something super vague, like "So, what's up?" which keeps you off balance about where to go with the convo.

Some people, unfortunately, will do whatever it takes to get ahead. They'll get away with as much as you don't audit, call out, or speak up on. You can't worry so much how it'll be received when you're fighting for yourself. I often ask myself, *What would a man do here?* Is a guy questioning which undercut to challenge and which not to? No! Any person with any power or status in business is always going to challenge something they don't feel right about. Your intuition will tell you when something is off, which is the nature of fighting like a girl.

PASS THE TORCH RIGHT BACK

Have you ever completely frozen up when someone challenged you unnecessarily or purposely threw you off your game with a pointed question? It happens to most of us when we think that these power players are more dominant and intelligent than they actually are. It's like we lose our words and can't find the right things to say (but of course the perfect response always comes *after* they've left the room). Sometimes the greatest way to challenge their power-hungry ways isn't overtly fighting back. Rather, you've got to understand their motivations and get inside their heads.

You can pass the torch back to men trying to intimidate you by asking them something that'll take them a minute to answer. Obviously, it'll depend on what exactly they're saying. But say, for example, someone asks something about your personal life to purposely throw you off. Something like "So, why are you single?" or "So, why don't you have kids?" It's the type of question that will immediately put you on the defensive (that's why it works).

If responding with a question of your own doesn't work in the situations you find yourself in, try repeating back the question getting sent your way. It'll give you an extra beat to think about a response that calls them on their shit, without it being a total blowup.

It also helps to have a rehearsed answer about why you don't answer certain questions about your personal life. If someone in a meeting asks you something that's outside the bounds of the conversation at hand, you can state directly, "You know, I'm not comfortable with that question. Let's move on." This will throw *them* off. Men especially have a tendency to say stupid shit, because they don't live in an emotional space. More times than not they'll respond by saying, "Oh, whoa, I'm sorry. I didn't realize that was wrong. I didn't mean to offend you." And you can respond with "Okay! Moving on" or "It takes a lot to offend me!" It makes the point and gives you the ability to control the situation.

THE SIXTY-SECOND RULE

Any time I'm nervous, I let myself feel scared, but only for a beat. You get to be nervous for one full minute. Leave the room if you have to. Let yourself feel every single emotion coursing through your body. Then put it the hell away and do you. Tell yourself that fear is a natural emotion, that you honored it, and that you now have to make space for your intuition to tell you what to do or say next.

OBSESSING OVER OUTCOME WILL RUIN YOUR ABILITY TO FIGHT

You can be vulnerable in business and your life, especially when you're fighting for something you're passionate about. It's a superpower to be able to soften in order to get what you want, without obsessing over your ability to get it. There's toughness in that. And strategy. However, what will never work is being fragile.

When you're fragile, it means that you can't receive difficult information. You can't handle not being chosen or deal with a particular tone. You can't hold your own when you're being questioned. When you showcase fragility to a client or person in power, you've immediately lost the fight. You'll be in the red immediately, and there's no winning there. *Not* handling it looks like taking things personally by making it about your inadequacies instead of getting back to business, and often manifests itself in tears, self-blame, and speaking in definites like "I can't do this anymore." Someone who's fragile internalizes external events that have nothing to do with them.

I've had major business meltdowns that simply wouldn't happen to me today because I was fragile then and cared too much about the outcome. The worst was this property on La Mesa in Santa Monica that nearly broke me. I became friends with a client and helped her buy a house over-looking the Riviera Country Club. It was on one of the best streets on the west side of LA. This property was going to be a lot of work, because there had been a ton of deferred maintenance on the home. She decided to proceed and was going to remodel the house. She was always unclear on whether she was going to live in it or flip it, and that's the biggest mistake you can make when remodeling a home. If you're going to sell it, you make every construction decision against the back-end numbers. You always keep your bottom line in mind. This woman wasn't doing that and spent in areas like fancy fixtures while disregarding the fucked plumbing. Who cares how beautiful your counters are if the toilet doesn't flush? After pouring money into this thing without any resale strategy, she decided she wanted to flip it. And like every awesome seller, she over-valued her home by 40 percent, because she was listening to her boyfriend, who was using comps from a totally different part of town. I said $16,995,000 and she said $23 million.

I had worked on this thing for so long that when I told them what I wanted to list it at, and they disagreed and threatened to give it to someone else, I took it at the number they wanted to sell it at . . . not the one I knew was right. I was too invested, to the point that I took every blow she gave me and kept telling myself that she would come around and get real about the number. Every time she wasn't happy with my response to our never-ending conversation about price, she threatened to release me from the listing and bring on a broker who believed in her home. Over the course of three years, I let this relationship hang over my head, and I was so fragile, afraid of losing the listing or, worse, that it would be sold by someone else at the number she wanted. I desperately wanted to prove myself. I was crying all the time, every problem with this one listing permeated my entire life, and I let it and her get to me.

In the end, I lost the listing and the years of blood, sweat, and (actual) tears that went into it. I let her see that fragile side of me. She knew I'd give in to whatever she wanted and allow us to do it her way even though I knew what was best. Instead, I should have compartmentalized rather than letting it permeate all parts of my existence. Decisions she was making about the state of that listing were affecting me in ways that were reactionary, personal, fragile, and ineffective. Ultimately, she ended up selling it for just over $15 million—landing under even what I thought it would trade at by close to a million.

Looking back, I knew from the beginning that I shouldn't have done this deal because the property was so grossly overpriced. But I was enchanted with how big a listing it was. I was attached to the idea that this would be my biggest one to date. I don't blame myself for that, though. Sometimes you have to obsess over outcomes (which, hi, is a fast track to fragility) in order to understand what red flags look like and what fights aren't ever going to be worth it.

Fragility is *needing* something to happen to prove your value or worth, like I did with that La Mesa property; vulnerability, on the other hand, is being honest about what your goals are. Wanting something, and being open enough to say that you want it, is vulnerability. People think that if they don't put it out there and claim what it is they want and are actually working toward, that will protect them and their feelings if it doesn't come to fruition. They think if they've admitted what they want, then it'll hurt ten times more if it doesn't happen. Whether you're speaking your truth to everybody or no one, it still exists inside you. It still hurts even if it doesn't turn out. It's just less of an ego blast, because other people don't get to see that you didn't get what you want.

Laser focus on outcomes gets in the way. You'll get punched square in the face if you're expecting to win everyone's approval and cross every finish line. I see it all the time. Attachments to money (especially). To the potential of a job promotion. To something a flaky client or colleague originally promised you. To the respect you wanted to win from a big-shot client. Obsessing over what we thought we were going to get is a fantasy that keeps us all in limbo. It makes us fragile because we're operating from a place of desperation, blinding our intuition and leaving us at risk of missing important cues.

What would happen if you told yourself at the outset of every meeting or conversation that the outcome does not determine your personal well-being or professional success? If some asshole cuts you off midsentence, or booms "I'm not happy" at you, or doesn't copy you on an email, silently tell yourself, *My life is not measured by the outcome of this fight.* You're going to fight like hell, for sure, but whether you win or lose does not determine your worth. You can't control every variable, and no one has a perfect hit rate. Assholes do not get to ruin your peace of mind. Don't allow it.

You've got to learn how to tolerate discomfort or you'll have no chance. You've got to go through the blows to learn how to be tougher. So if you're not feeling that way now, do things that will allow you to learn it. Take a boxing class and start from the outside in. Do a boot camp. Make yourself vulnerable to feedback at a stand-up comedy class. Even when certain power plays freak you out, knowing they don't have any real power over you helps you stay light on your toes and allows you to muster the courage to fight back. It's not easy. I've been on both sides of this before. Fighting matters.

WHAT NOT TO DO

Aside from not taking any more shit, there are some things I just won't do when I fight. They're non-negotiables for me. While I'm more protective of myself and my emotional state, and more outspoken because of it, there are some ways people will intimidate in order to control a situation that I simply don't agree with. No matter how pissed I get, I won't lie, play dirty, or disparage their name.

> ***Don't lie.*** Whether it's my personal life or my professional life, I don't want to lie. I'm not a good liar, number one. And I would rather make you hear something that makes you uncomfortable. That's how I put my head on the pillow at night. Stick to the truth; otherwise you muddy the waters, which makes it hard to be effective. You'll always be wondering what you said or trying to recover from something you got caught doing. If you operate from that place, you're less confident in your ability to communicate. Be completely honest, and you never have to worry about it coming back to you. When you're coming from that place, you never have to ask, *God, who did I tell that to?* Now, omitting is another

story. Not every person needs all the details. As any good lawyer would say, *you don't blow your wad in the beginning.* You want to have ammunition when you need it. They don't need to know all of your cards.

Don't play dirty. In my business it's very competitive, and everyone has been screwed over at some point. It's when that happens that *some* people say, *You know what? Fuck this. I'm going to play dirty too.* It's a really, really fine line, because when you get taken, it gets a little easier to justify screwing over someone else. My personal philosophy is that I'm never going to play dirty; I'm going to fight right in the open where everyone can see. I'm not going to make any apologies for that, either. Recently, a friend and colleague of mine, Paul, had a listing that was pretty big. For a variety of reasons, it didn't work out, and the seller came to me to list the property after the listing was canceled. Meaning I now have his business. I'm not going to make any apologies for taking a listing from Paul, because the seller pursued me. I know he's disappointed, and we had a long conversation about it, and I won't be apologizing. I wouldn't feel okay with it if I had pursued the listing behind my friend's back. Or a colleague's back. That's how it goes in the lion's den out there—a lot of people will play dirty, and a lot of those people are very successful. But I'm not sure that they are resting well at night, and if they are, bless. Karma is a patient little gangster. You always have to be aware of that and your surroundings and make a choice ahead of time that you're not going to give in to that kind of dirty play.

Don't disparage anyone's name. There will be plenty of chances to intentionally get ahead by keeping your competition back: by saying shitty things about them or putting them down to others or trying to minimize them. You can't do it. And I won't. Sometimes people will try to put you into the corner, like they're baiting you to speak poorly about someone else to prove your own worth in the situation.

This just happened to me yesterday with the new listing I got that used to be Paul's. The owners of the property told me how many buyers Paul had brought to the listing in order to show it and said, "What do you think about that,

Tracy? Do you think that's a good amount of showings for a little over a year?"

"I'm not going to disparage the previous agent," I said. "And to answer you, no. I don't think six showings is enough." I wasn't going to speak about Paul and his business and whatever he did or didn't do. I just need to do better.

He replied, "That's why you're here. You're going to do it better." He said it, not me. I didn't have to take down my colleague and friend in order to get the truth out there.

Actually say "I don't want to disparage [their name]" *out loud*. The only exception is if you *do* think they're a scumbag and that *is* the reputation of someone you're dealing with. (There are very few times when I will say that unless it's completely true. Don't recommend someone who's scum; that'll reflect poorly on you, too.)

I know that if I want to work with people who are respectful of me down the road, I want to showcase that I'm going to live up to that. I'm simply not going to speak badly about someone I respect or like, no matter how much someone wants me to. When you're pitching and winning business, you don't always know who you're going up against. So in that situation, and most situations, it's easier to focus on you and your skill set without bringing your competition into it. You can differentiate yourself and make your case without bringing someone down while you do.

In real estate, having relationships with brokers (some of whom are my competition) is as crucial to my success as my relationships with clients. In any business, you need to collaborate. And if you can't, it'll hurt you. I don't always get this right. Recently I went into a listing appointment where the client told me he was really disappointed that one of my colleagues (okay, it was David Parnes) didn't come to meet him for the listing. David referred him to another agent in Pasadena because he didn't want to deal with it. The seller was talking to me about how much David was his *faaavorite* person on the show, *blah blah blah*, and I was offended. Unfortunately, I showed it. Because he was legit saying, "I'm glad you came, but I do wish it was David instead."

My response was "Look, I came all the way here with my partner on a busy day to meet you. David pawned you off on a local agent because he didn't care to deal with you. And David doesn't get out of bed for less than $10 million." *Whoops.* Slid right out. But I was pissed. It took me an hour to get there. I'm sitting in front of him, and he has the nerve to bring up his preference for my competition. I mean, number one, you are lucky that *I* drove out here for this. Number two, I have sat with you at the folding card table in your kitchen for an hour talking about a cohesive marketing plan and staging for a house that will sell quickly if we put the right price on it. And number three—unrelated—you are a creepy fan dude who is talking about my costar like you want to sleep with him, not list your house.

In reality, though, my response was not intended to disparage David but rather to point out to Creepy Seller Guy that I actually got into the car and drove here. David ended up confronting me because Creepy Seller Guy told him what I had said, which you know he did to get him there, and it worked. But what I had said was completely true, and I told David that. I said in candor, "Look, I spoke the truth, which was that you didn't come to Pasadena and I did. You better believe that was my response to the owner because it was the truth. I love you, but I'm not going to sit in front of some guy and not claim that I'm the better fit for the job because I'm *there* when you physically pawned it off on a junior manager in Pasadena." I didn't have to worry about having spoken facts about my competition, even if they were framed as disparaging, because it was 100 percent the truth and I could be anchored in that when my words got back to me. Bottom line—David didn't get in the car and drive to Pasadena until I said what I said, and he was getting that listing because my big mouth got in the way.

I learned a really valuable lesson, though. I let that guy get me on the defensive and in turn I made it more about my competitor than I probably should have. I should have said, "We shouldn't discuss my colleague when we are meeting. I did show up. I did drive. I did come here for you and your mother's house. And I would appreciate if we focus on me. My time is valuable, so let's get back to the comps." Instead I got stuck. I only got halfway there, which made it about my competition, when in fact I should have confronted the man in front of me, not David, who wasn't there. In the end Creepy Seller Guy offered his favorite cast member the listing and they lived happily ever after. And all I have to show for it is a lesson.

Chapter 4

....

GET
GRITTY

*M*y friend Cory always says that I'm the person who doesn't let a fish get away once it's been hooked. Even if it finds a way to unhook itself in the water before I reel it in, I'll get off the goddamn raft, dive headfirst into the water, and swim to catch it with my bare hands if I have to. *No way, little fucker.* I do it in every deal, no matter what, which is why more times than not I win. Because I'm not willing to let something just die. I will try every possible way to get a deal done before I give up on it.

That's the part of grit that most people don't totally get—you don't always do the same thing over and over and over again to endure and come out on the other side (hopefully with a win). Rather, you persevere because you choose to come at situations with a new approach. You're willing to take any strategy or angle in order to succeed, not just the one that you've been trying. Grit is a lightness on your toes that will help you keep coming up with new strategies and inhabiting alternate perspectives until one of them works. Look, I know it can be downright exhausting when you're in a situation that you just want to be over and done with. That's when you resign yourself to the problem instead of being creative and strategic about how to solve what you're facing. You're inadvertently extending your misery. In this chapter you'll learn how to be resourceful when you're completely maxed out, and I'll teach you how to *just survive* when the most important thing is staying in the game. Because I've been there.

Up until this point, I've taught you to confront people when they try to give you shit. But there are some people, clients, situations, and even full stages of existence that you can't just break up with. Sometimes, unfortunately, you've just got to take it. There will always be things outside your control—blowups, frustrations, and bad moods—that have nothing to do with you. Most people aren't after you, which is why it's not productive to fight with them every chance you get. It'll wear you down even further and not lead to the outcome you hope. Plus, some people have so much influence and power that enduring their nonsense for a period of time could be worth it (if it's getting you a bigger trade-off). That's really what hanging in there is all about—you knowing what's more important to you than the situation at hand.

Maybe you took a job with a manager who could help you learn a new skill set in your industry, but that boss is a drag to work with. You regret your job choice, and you're drained by having to be around them every day. An option would be to stop and course-correct to a new role. To leave. But if you know that your bigger goal is to get out of your comfort zone and learn something new, and you feel that, despite their terrible mood, you're learning what you came there to learn, it may be worth sticking with it until you've developed the skill set that originally brought you there.

Or maybe you took on a client you're not a fan of on a personal level, but you did it because they're a superconnector. They know everyone and could help you bring in a ton of future business. Unfortunately, though, they're that type who has to be the smartest person in the room—and they do that by making everyone around them feel dumb. It makes you second-guess your own intelligence and overall brings up insecurities every time you're around them. After a few months of this, or even a few weeks, if you're feeling like you can barely do your work well, you have to come back to your original goal: to get new business from them. But if you can't succeed for them because of how they're making you feel, then maybe you should part ways. If you can, it might be worth tolerating their BS to massively extend your network and get a ton of new business. Always come back to the trade-offs and whether they're working for you.

If your first instinct is to get mad, blow it all up, and quit, I get it. Listen, I have those days, too. Then I'll get a fire in my eye and remember that it's time to let it roll off my back. It's a whole new day, and I'm not going to let this take me down. It's up to me to bring personality and energy to the rooms I'm in, even if I'm up to my eyeballs in bullshit from a crazy client or a failing marriage or trolls coming at me online. You don't get to quit life.

BEING RESOURCEFUL WHEN YOU'RE EXHAUSTED

The Altmans, my costars on the show, recently brought me on to help with a listing that wasn't getting the client's asking price of $9 million. They're busy in their business, too, and they needed a fresh set of eyes to talk to the clients and hopefully bring a new network of brokers and potential buyers to the listing. It soon became clear to me that the seller needed to be told that the house was a fixer. Despite the fact that it was maintained well, with finishes that were only twenty years old instead of fifty, every surface needed to be touched. I brought up all the little things that the seller had been looking past. He understood that the bathroom tile needed to be updated, but he didn't get the little things, like the bull-nosed countertops and how the walls had rounded edges (another dated finish). The house was also on a wonky plot of land, even though the street and the neighborhood were great. Because of this, I suggested a $500,000 price reduction to $8.5 million. In the first week, we ended up getting multiple offers—one from a neighbor and one from a developer—but both in the low $7 million range. The seller didn't think that was high enough, so the deals were sorta dead in the water.

But one of the potential buyers, the developer, was a client of mine, so I sat down with him and said, "Look, this seller really wants eight for this." Now, before I go on, you have to understand that when you're in a dual agency, meaning you're representing both parties, the stakes are incredibly high. You risk having one or both parties think that you're not on their side. They could question your integrity and put your whole reputation at risk if they believe you didn't represent them well. It's a tricky situation that requires incredible finesse. I needed to get this negotiation right, because my reputation is everything.

So I said to the developer buyer/client of mine: "What if—because you know you're going to flip this at $11 or $12 million once you're done with it—we create a sliding scale on the back end? You'll throw him $200K for every million more you make on it." I was doing this so that we could get new traction. Everyone knows that the longer something sits on the market, the worse off everyone involved is.

Offering up a sliding-scale alternative isn't a typical thing to do. But sometimes that's what tough situations call for. If you're struggling to think outside the box with a problem you're facing, you need to get yourself out of your own situation. Leave the problem or go for a walk or call someone outside the situation who has enough industry knowledge to help you think of something different. In this case, the idea struck me in a quiet moment, and luckily it worked.

Part of grit is getting creative in order to endure, which comes up in all types of situations, industries, businesses, and deals.

You can use grit when you feel like you're tapped out on how to make a situation better with a boss or colleague. You can get creative with a client or customer who seems to have a never-ending list of problems. It'll require doing something that's perhaps not industry standard (like negotiating a contract point that's usually fixed but doesn't actually have to be) or attempting to be more direct with someone on your team than you've ever been before. If you're a little scared to take a new approach, that's probably the one you should take. Anyplace you have ongoing, continual stress that you'd rather ditch than deal with, changing your perspective, viewpoint, or strategy can help you get a new result.

"NO" DOESN'T ALWAYS MEAN "NO"

I tell my younger team members all the time that you can turn a "no" to a "yes" if you can expose the vulnerability in the other party's position. You just have to take a peek at the cards they're trying to hold close to their chest and see what they have to lose.

One of my agents, Rob, was recently helping my best friend buy a house that was in escrow (the third party that's in charge of managing the documents and deposit that are coming from buyers and sellers during the course of a real estate deal). When it came time for inspections, it turned out this twenty-year-old condo had a bunch of maintenance and repairs it needed to the hardware, flooring, and walls. The whole thing was going to cost $15,000, and the seller responded by offering my friend a $7,000 credit. They should've been covering the whole thing, if you ask me.

My buyer (and best friend) was calling me asking if she should really let this deal go over $8,000 and give up this condo that she really wanted. Rob reported back that it was a flat "no": "Well, they said this is *it*. It is this or nothing."

I told him to hold on. I reminded Rob that last time we were in the condo, there were boxes everywhere. They were already packed, which meant *they* were the ones in the vulnerable position. They needed this more than we did. So I told him he had room to go back and try to get more money, because it clearly wasn't a closed door yet. Sure enough, that's what he did and got another $4,000 in credit for my friend.

This is learnable. You just have to be willing to see the window cracked open that you could get through when everyone else is so focused on a locked door. I'm always looking for the hole. The best way to figure out where that is is by asking a lot of questions of people you're working with. The more information you have, the more you're able to see who's vulnerable and why. Trust me, people love to talk, and they don't realize how much they're sharing with you until it's too late and you're able to use it to your advantage. This can be used everywhere in your life to get what you want. For instance:

- When you want to negotiate a new job offer (ask, "Is there room to negotiate?")

- When doing a sponsorship deal (ask, "Do you have a budget in mind?")
- When creating a partnership between two businesses (ask, "What's your biggest concern?")
- When you're in a one-on-one with your boss (ask, "What problems are you facing that I'm not privy to?")

STAYING OPTIMISTIC

There are times when I've shown up to meetings feeling like, *I'd rather die than be in a room with you. But I'm here. I'm not excited to be here, because I dislike you immensely. But I'm here.* That, however, is *not* what I encourage you to think. It'll only make you feel worse when your bad energy produces a bad outcome.

Being on *Million Dollar Listing*, I simply don't have any choice but to bring "the personality," even when I'm not feeling like it. I've never *not* been feeling it more than when I had to shoot four days a week while I was in the middle of moving out of the home that I'd raised my family in. It was chaos. But I'm being paid to be on television. If you're watching *Million Dollar Listing Los Angeles* and don't like the Altmans, you might like the Brits. If you don't like Flagg, maybe you respond to Madison. With me, you either love me or hate me. Which is pretty true for my life in general—you either have a flavor for me or you don't. On the show, it gives me no choice. My full energy is crucial, even more so because I feel like there's a microscope on me as the only woman as a primary cast member.

I've fucked this up a hundred times. I've had low energy when I needed to bring my full force. I've not delivered when I needed to deliver, which is my job. And it's been my fault. It's particularly hard for me in the interviews, because I don't get to interact with anyone else. But even that has taught me focus—that in order to fully feel like myself when all the balls are in the air and I have a million things going on and I have to deliver, I've got to be fully there in order to do well. I can't afford to be distracted by feeling like shit. I have to just show up with as much energy as the show needs that day until I get it right.

For you, low energy might come at the exact time you need it most because you were up with a screaming baby before your presentation was due. Or you heard a sexist comment just before you walked into a big pitch meeting. If this happens to you—feeling negative and tired and frustrated right when you need the exact opposite—the easiest thing you can do in the moment is take five deep breaths. No one will see it. You don't have to leave the situation. But it'll reset your nervous system. This happens to all of us, especially when we're in situations where we need to impact the outcome. I'm a master at compartmentalizing, which helps me persevere through some tough days when I'd really rather be anywhere but where I am. You've got to learn to put it out of sight and out of mind, which can be hard. Consider these quickies I often employ to trick myself into a more positive state of mind:

- If you have time, work out, even if it's just for ten minutes. Use happy hormones to your advantage. Works every time.
- Read some of your favorite inspirational quotes (I save mine whenever I see them on Instagram to go back to on tough days). Here are some of my favorites that boost my mood:
  - "Never water yourself down because someone can't handle you at 100 proof."
  - "I stopped waiting for the light at the end of the tunnel and lit that bitch up myself."
  - "Baby girl, breathe and remind yourself of who the fuck you are."
  - "You are either at the table or on the menu."
- Blast music in the car. With the windows up. Not down, never down.

- Vent to a partner or friend. Send one unedited, ferocious text saying absolutely everything you need to. Get it off your chest so you can move through it and move on.
- Don't dwell on it once you've finished venting. The more you talk about it, the more it'll creep into the parts of your life if doesn't need to be in. That's why when I shoot, for example, my team knows I can't afford to have a nasty client sucking the life out of me. I'm trying to give everything I have to the producers. Staying present in the moment will help shield yourself from other energy-sucking areas of your life.

People are going to be important in developing your grit. But none will be more important than you and your mind-set. You've got to be tough or you won't cut it in the rooms you're vying to get in (which, by the way, get harder and filled with more difficult personalities). You'll be walking out, which is the opposite of what you need to do. You want to stay there until you've won. You just have to keep going. That's it. Keep putting up with it if it's important to you.

THREE CUPS OF COFFEE AND TWO GLASSES OF ROSÉ

Look, you're going to go through shit. You're going to feel like shit. You're going to have days where the last fucking thing you want to do is show up with a smile on your face. Sometimes grit just means having the self-awareness to reach for (relatively) healthy coping mechanisms that'll keep you from being totally miserable while you wait it out.

Let's just say the only way I've learned to sort it out is with three cups of coffee and two glasses of rosé. It depends on my mood. You better believe I'm the only cast member who needs a bottle of rosé on the sideboard. Luckily, there's a whole team of people around me most times we shoot (except during interviews) to help me bring my full personality to the table.

I deal with all kinds of crazy people who make me want to quit the business, but I've never encountered anyone like Ice Pick Guy. This client was a real piece of work. We had his home in Bel Air under contract, and everything was blowing up over Christmas. It looked like it was going to fall out, so I did what any good agent does and tried to bring the buyer and seller together . . . a little give-and-take

is important when the stakes are high. Unfortunately, my client did not agree with my sentiment and went off the rails.

At this point I would have preferred acid in *my* bleeding sockets over talking any further with him. But wait, it keeps going . . .

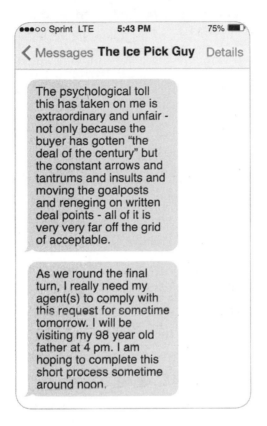

Listen, I absolutely hear his plea and candidly agree that the buyer was unreasonable and shifty to say the least. But the barrage of texts went on for days. Seventy-five completely unhinged back-and-forths (I'll spare you the rest). I mean, come on, dude, let's slow our roll on the crazy train. But as I've done so many times, I was forced to take the bullshit in order to get the deal done. And as much as I love being the subject of my client's internal rage, these over-the-top emotions are just too much sometimes. The client was desperately depending on me, and every day the house didn't sell, he'd send me a text explaining how much money he'd just lost. It got to the point that every time the phone made a noise, I was filled with anxiety and dread that it was him. This was a great family in a really shitty situation, and even wonderful people in bad spots can be assholes. I even went so far as to give him his own ringtone so I knew when my phone made a noise whether it was him or not.

So I had to bring in Gina, a senior partner on my team, to start dealing with him. It was the biggest relief, because I had help to offset his emotional instability. We'd trade off, because neither of us could handle his crazy on our own. At some point it makes *you* feel crazy. I could have not asked her for help, but I'm so glad I did, because I probably wouldn't have been able to get that deal done and that guy out of my life without someone else enduring with me. I'd have been miserable if I didn't have someone I could laugh with about this nuts behavior. That's the whole point of it, right? You share in your failures and you share in your successes. You're much better, whether things are terrible or wonderful, when there are friends or colleagues around. You can share the burden of dealing with an exhausting person with a colleague who's less emotionally invested. Try having someone read your emails first if you're dreading opening them because you know they're toxic. Or avoid spending time alone with a terrible boss by asking someone on your team to come along for the casual coffee the boss invited you to. Having trusted colleagues act as middlemen and help off-load the stress of tough situations is the only way I can get through some terrible chapters of life.

WHAT'S WORTH IT?

One of my favorite coping mechanisms is reminding myself that I only have to endure a difficult person for a limited amount of time. A one-hour meeting. A week-long conference, after which I'll be in a bubble bath with a glass of wine. A two-year slog to sell a $100 million property, after which I'll never work with someone that difficult again.

Sometimes, however, in going through this exercise, I realize that the "limited" amount of time is actually too much time given the personal costs. I now make a practice of sitting down with myself and deciding what I won't—and shouldn't—endure. When I've gotten myself into a tough partnership of any kind—with a team member, a friend, a relationship, a client—I ask myself what I'm willing to handle and for how long. If you can put a name to what you're dealing with, and a time line, then you can check in with yourself to see if this situation is still one you want to engage in. Every personality has a price, but the only way to figure that price out is to go through it. You'll learn what you can tolerate *and to what end.* If I'm not making enough money to offset the cost to my health and stability, it's not worth it. Trust your instincts on when that's the case. You'll know. We always know.

Right now, there actually is a property that I'm taking a beating on. Hey, it's $100 million, so my tolerance level is higher. But I knew two minutes into our first meeting that making this much money would come at a cost, because I instinctively knew the kind of personality type that was sitting across from me in the room. He had a reputation that preceded him (per his own words). I had a lot of conversations with myself and with my team about what it meant to engage with this personality. My current endgame in this situation is a potential $10 million in the next two years.

Here's how I try to decide if the endgame of a situation is worth the cost:

- Am I perpetually unhappy in order to see it through?
- Is my health suffering? (Am I getting run down?)
- Am I losing sleep for days or weeks on end?

- Have I set and exceeded a personal time line for dealing with this situation?

Early on, I decided two years was too long to deal with this guy. I'm subjected to every whim, concern, and random thought that enters his mind. He has a negative attitude, and he won't loosen his grip on me and my team. He fires and rehires me. He's a bully and an egomaniac. I determined that if I don't see a certain trust being born and a respect for what I am bringing to the table, then I'll find an exit on my terms. I'm already assessing what I can tolerate and for how long (if we even make it there).

In my business, a lot of what you decide to tolerate depends on how much you need the paycheck. I mean, that's true in any business. For any of us. We're all at different places, stages, and backgrounds in our life, and what we'll tolerate for certain amounts of money is a totally necessary conversation. And the answer will change depending on where we're at in our careers. In the beginning of mine, I dealt with crap on small listings. Now, to deal with that same type of personality, there really needs to be another zero on that listing price. Sometimes you'll require that an opportunity—like a speaking gig, a promotion, or a side hustle—pay better if you can see it's going to involve some crazy personalities, because those involved are possibly detrimental to your well-being. It better pay more than it was paying before, if money is the trade-off that's worth it to you (that could also be visibility, résumé building, connections, etc.).

If you do decide to see something through, for any amount of time, play hardball and set the tone in the relationship. There's nothing more empowering than saying what you need to someone who's constantly trying to undercut it. Persisting doesn't mean you take it quietly and do whatever the hell someone says. It means that you speak up, you hold your boundaries, you ask for what you need, you say exactly what's on your mind . . . until the very end. If you continuously check in with yourself on what that end is, what needs to happen, or what needs to change, you'll stay in full control of yourself and your truth and, in turn, the relationship. Because you'll know your trade-offs, why you're doing it, and what you're getting out of it. If you do that, no matter who makes the call, you'll have won.

NO HANDOUTS HERE

Failure is always an opportunity to learn, rather than a final statement on your potential. Over the years, I've built my business on being psycho about putting deals together—no matter what. I never took "no" for an answer. I still don't, and I never assumed it was all just going to fall in my lap. I

see this with some of the young agents in this business—
believing that it will all just come their way. I thought that
too at the beginning of my career, but damn, I couldn't have
been more wrong. And the only way you learn how wrong
you are is by having the rug ripped out from beneath you.

Even my sister's house, which I am launching soon, is
something that I've had to work my ass off for two decades
in order to deserve. Funny, because when she first bought
it a decade ago, I thought I deserved to be the agent on it
then. You might be thinking, *Well, lucky you. It's your sister's house! Obviously she is going to work with you.* Not exactly. Nothing in my career has come as easily as you might
think (or I might have hoped). I've been hustling in Los
Angeles for almost twenty years to work up to a listing this
valuable when it comes to the market. My sister wasn't doing me any favors!

Ten years ago, when she first bought the home for $13.5
million, it would have been one of my biggest deals at that
time in my career . . . *if* she had used me as her real estate
agent. But that's not what happened. When I learned that
she had bought it through someone else and hadn't even
asked me, I nearly quit the business. I kept saying to myself,
If my own family doesn't see my value, who the hell will? Losing my sister's business took a couple years to recover from.
It took even longer for me to realize the value in that loss.

Instead of quitting, I let the lesson and pain of that

experience drive me. I now look back and see the mistakes I made, and I can be honest with myself that I wasn't in a place to put in the time, investment, and hustle that I do today. Now here we are a decade later and her listing will be mine . . . and *now* I have the skill set, the business acumen, and the team to handle both this listing and others just like it. This time around I deserve it, but not because it fell in my lap. I deserve it because I'm the grittiest agent she knows, who happens to be quite charming. Nothing within the confines of a deal could faze me, and I know how to outsmart whatever competition we're facing. I know that now, which is why I'm successful. But not even my sister's listing would be mine if that weren't the case.

Not getting my sister's listing was a humbling experience, but it set me on the path that we all need to be on— you've got to persevere through a lot of situations in order to end up on top and in order to do business at the highest levels of your industry. It required me to look at my connections and relationships not just as guarantees but as possibilities. So I started getting out there. Instead of assuming things were in the bag for me (as I had with my sister's original listing), I started doing everything possible to build relationships. I had arrogance at one time, but then I got that great proverbial slap in the face. I woke up. Do I sometimes wish it all came easier for me? Of course. But since I've put in the work to gain people's trust over a long period of time professionally, and I've shown not just myself but the world what I'm capable of, now it's obvious to people who to go to. But that wasn't always the case. I had to choose to keep going to *prove* that . . . even when people thought I was unproven. I take these tough situations and I examine them. It's the best way to ensure you *actually* learn from what you've gone through. If you're slapped in the face by a "no," once the sting wears off, think through these questions:

- What can I do in the future to keep from this happening again?
- What's one thing I learned about myself from this giant-ass "no"?
- Where did I make an assumption and why did I make that assumption?

Don't live your life with the fear that everyone else is always right but with the confidence that you will be, eventually.

Chapter 5

LIGHTEN UP AND WIN

*S*o many people suck. Come on, you know it's true. But if you can learn to lighten up and lay one out there, especially when everyone is being *very* serious, you'll always be able to control the room in your favor (not to mention, you'll be the person everyone wants to be around). If you can hit a joke here and there, you'll want to keep reading. If you can't, not sure what to do with you. Kidding. A little bit.

Lightness, whether you're the one delivering it or the one laughing at it, is a key indicator of someone who's self-assured, because it requires vulnerability. You won't always be funny every time you try, but you won't be scared of that fact either. It comes with the territory. Plus, get a super serious group of people around a table to laugh at a time when it seems impossible, and you'll have more power to control the situation than you realize.

Bringing humor to the table has helped me during some pretty dark times. It's made certain awful clients manageable. And my divorce less hellish. It's helped me help friends through some really tough chapters. It's also gotten me into trouble (more on that later). I get that not everyone is funny or, like me, had to rely on being boisterous and entertaining to be seen since the time they were a kid. I've been using humor for what feels like my whole life. I was the eighth-grade class clown who was insecure growing up and used this knack for humor (which, honestly, has just always been there for me) to make up for being a little squirt. Seriously, I was tiny—barely five feet tall entering high school. So I made my personality *that* much bigger. I was the last ninth grader in the city of Los Angeles to get my period (I'd put my money on it), and I didn't get boobs until I was, like, fifteen. So I got people's attention by making them laugh. I'm not sure that I'm any funnier now than I was then, but now my humor comes from a much more authentic place. I'm not making up for anything anymore, and I don't take anything nearly as seriously—myself included.

Which, in my opinion, is the sign of confident humor. It's when you can use jokes and wit to bring people together and to lighten the mood, instead of using them to be seen. It's less about shock and awe and more about the gift of lightness to the people who may need it most. If you can get people to laugh, you're immediately going to be able to move the situation where you want. It'll be like a little crack in the facade of intensity that not only makes the situation more manageable but will break the intensity of everything going on—in work, in life, in love. You name it.

Professionally, I've always found that walking into listing appointments can be very intense, and humor can help show your strength. After one of the biggest listing appointments of my life, a client said, "I'm a beast. I'm not sure you can handle this." I responded, "Growing up, my dad answered the phone with 'What do you want?' I have this in spades." When someone throws that kind of shade (and ego) your way, the only way to respond is with equal intensity, while also making light of it. Humor can disarm. Otherwise they'll think that they're succeeding at intimidating you. Your joke can show that's not the case. Someone who wasn't me might have taken offense at that comment, or gotten quiet, or asked what he meant. Any of those things would have given power to the comment. Well-timed lightness can immediately suck the intimidation out of the attempt—and put you back in control.

It can be scary to use humor, because you're exposing yourself, and because it sucks when people don't get your jokes. Even if they're not always received well, you just have to try it. Even if it doesn't always land, you don't have to get uncomfortable and weird about it. I always try it, and maybe for that reason some people don't take me as seriously. I couldn't tell you why I don't get certain listings. Maybe it's because of that. But I generally find it more helpful than not, because humor is such a core way that people connect—by laughing at the same thing—and because it shows I can mean business and still have fun. There's seriously nothing that can break an overly icy room, or powerful personality types, better than a joke that gets everyone to stop taking the situation seriously. There are a few different types of humor that work best in different situations, and some that I find myself using more than others. Humor has many faces. Use the right one in the right way, and your fear will be kept at bay and your power maximized.

SELF-DEPRECATING HUMOR

With the right audience, this always works. With most audiences, throwing a joke out there before a meeting about being hungry, or sweating, typically lands. Poking fun at yourself can be a great bridge to show people you don't take yourself too seriously to see the fun in the situation. I use this one a lot. I like to call out obvious shit happening, like when I'm inappropriately dressed (like that time I showed up to a construction site in heels, or my kid's soccer game in full hair and makeup; it's ridiculous, and I know it). When you do this, you're giving people permission to laugh at you. There's always an opportunity to poke fun at yourself in a way that lightens the mood without beating yourself up. You've got to know who you're talking to, understand that audience, and throw in a joke accordingly. It's not scripted, but it's always there.

Being self-deprecating and funny about the differences between you and who you're around is also a really great way to build a bridge. It's warm, and it's apologetic. And it connects. You can show that you're doing you, and they're doing them, and neither of you is the other person. I'd call out our differences. Acknowledging how different your world is from theirs is a way of showing that you're good enough with yourself to find it hilarious how different you are from them. Owning those differences is such an easy way to find humor in a situation and to appreciate a room full of differences (which makes it the most interesting room to be in). Look for that bridge, especially when you're feeling totally opposite of the people you're with. What doesn't make sense to you is humorous in and of itself. It's a great way to relate to differences in a way that brings everyone together.

UNIVERSAL HUMOR

When there are questions you can't answer, or terribly awkward moments, these are great and unifying moments to say something funny. Universal humor is that common thread that everyone can relate to. They'll understand. I think the dynamics between men and women, and their differences, are always funny and something that everyone relates to no matter their gender or sexuality. You get it. Relationships are always easy to find the humor in. Throwaway comments—like the little under-your-breath thoughts that everyone is already thinking—are typically unifying and always funny when you're the person to actually say it out loud.

This is my favorite to use when I can see a situation going in a direction that might really be heading south. On a recent trip, one of my girlfriends had to go home early because her dad was sick and in the hospital. She was dealing with her kids, telling them that they all had to go home early, and I could tell she was on the brink of tears. I needed to lighten the mood or she was going to start bawling, which is fine but not what I knew she wanted in that moment. The problem was that she was dealing with her ten-year-old daughter, who did not want to go home. She's ten. I totally get it. But my girlfriend was getting increasingly bummed that her daughter wasn't getting that a family member was in the hospital. I could see the tension rising and knew she was going to snap if I didn't do something.

So as her daughter was wailing about how she was losing five whole days of her vacation, I started poking fun at the timing and going on an absurd tangent about how it was four days, not five, and lucky her because of that. I started counting the days and hours and taking the whole thing too far, until they were both laughing at how ridiculous I was being. It was totally stupid and a throwaway joke that everyone was thinking but no one was saying because emotions were running so high. But it worked. It redirected that negative energy, kept my girlfriend from blowing, and calmed her daughter down. When you see something heading south, whether in a situation like this or at dinner with two people who are about to go down a dark, fighting path, stepping in with a universal joke that's goofy can keep everyone from totally losing it.

DEFENSIVE HUMOR

This is humor that's negative and cutting. To me, it's the worst kind of humor, but it can be used effectively, and sometimes it's needed. There's always some sort of truth that's being masked in humor. It's that one-liner that's as cutting as it is honest, but you're masking it in some sarcastic comment. Yes, people are going to laugh, but it's not from a positive place. You've probably been on the receiving end of one of these jokes. I have. It doesn't feel good, which is why it's never my go-to.

However, some people require defensive humor—the people who are very difficult to disarm and the people who likely use sarcasm themselves. You've got to make sure they understand that they're not going to get to you. They'll try to come at you from every angle and kick you off balance, and if you can come back at them with a similar but more playful jab, you'll remind them that you can't be fucked with, but it'll be masked in sarcasm and humor. I had a client who was trying to bully me and giving me a whole lot of shit for "looking nervous." It was Intimidation 101, and he was trying to make me feel insecure. It's in those moments, when you want to punch back and say "fuck you," that something a bit more sarcastic works far better than lashing out. When you lash out, it shows that they got to you. So instead, I looked at him and said, "There's not an ounce of me that's nervous, shug." I let my patronizing comment be humorous without being cruel. In any of your relationships, you don't want your humor to go to *too* cutting a place, because it's just mean. Plus, it will affect them and how they perceive you.

With abrasive personality types, defensive humor can be both your shield and your weapon. When there's no sense of warmth from them, and you're living in their space and subjected to their jabs, it's the only way to throw them off balance. It's important that you do, because it keeps you from looking weak, which is what these huge personality types thrive on. If you have a really quick comeback with people like that, they know there's not a crack in your fucking shield. This humor is the hardest because it's such a fine line. You don't want to be too abrasive, and you also don't want to be too guarded. But with some trial and error, you'll get it right, and you'll show them that you're strong and you're not going to cry. You can hang, and a little comeback shows that. It's hard to get ahead when you're always on the defensive, but with those big egos and aggressive personalities that are, unfortunately, so common in my business, this humor doesn't lighten the mood as much as it shows you can handle it (and signals to them to *cut it out*).

Similarly, in the right situations, defensive humor can keep you from cracking, because you're defending yourself from your own reality. When I was going through my divorce, my attorney was on the receiving end of my jabs all the time. I was saying all kinds of dumb shit when we were in mediation. I would joke with him about needing to turn his hearing aid up: "Can you even hear what's going on in there?" He would laugh right along with me, because I was being playful when we both knew that I was a wreck. I was irritated as hell going through this, and I just wanted to get it over with. I could have gone down the path of anger, but instead I made light of the entire situation by making fun of my attorney when the mediation was getting tense. It helped me get through it, and we both knew it was better than what my unbridled anger would have done. This was defensive humor, poking fun at someone else, who was pretty aware of himself to begin with. In situations like that, it totally works without being cold.

Some people would say there's a time and a place for humor. And they're probably right. There are some moments I don't use my humor at all—especially when we're selling a house and it's a divorce, someone has died, or it's truly an emotionally challenging situation. I've had situations where you walk into what feels like the dead middle of a gray cloud. You can cut the tension with a knife. Sometimes it requires me to become assistant, therapist, friend, and real estate agent. In these heavy situations, most people would say humor doesn't have a place. But if you very clearly pick your moments, you can be a huge asset by lightening a really heavy room with humor. The best humor to use in these situations is self-deprecating humor (poking a bit of fun at yourself) or finding something truly funny about the situation. Being vulnerable enough to find a way to brighten their day with a quick laugh can really help someone during difficult times.

Yes, even your humor can be strategized. But more than anything, you just have to have the confidence to try it. Humor isn't careful. It's always a little bit risky. It's in the uncomfortable moments that it's truly the funniest. If it does land, you've got someone in your corner for sure. If it doesn't land, don't get uncomfortable and weird about it, because it won't always be that way. And if you take it too far, well . . . I've been there.

REEL IT BACK

The only way you know if your joke goes too far is by going too far. There's no way around it. The risk of saying something funny is that it isn't funny at all. And at its worst, it upsets someone. Both of which have happened to me. But you learn how to land jokes much like you learn how to ride a bike—by striking the balance found only from losing your balance . . . and falling. Want to know how you know you've taken it too far? The room goes quiet. That's how.

Unfortunately for me, I took a joke too far with a guy who I'm fairly sure is mafia. No joke: if you google him, he's definitely a tough guy. When he was buying one of my listings, the whole deal was totally convoluted and complicated. We were on a conference call, and I was referencing the size of the house, what the square footage was inside and out. He had a million questions and we were going back and forth. In the context of my response, I said, "Don't be stupid. It's fine, I told you." I used the phrase lightly and jokingly, but it sent him over the edge. The conversation was playful enough that I thought I could say that. I *really* misjudged. That was the end of that conversation. Immediately he shut it down. I was caught so off guard. Then his agent called me shortly afterward to say that I needed to apologize. *Are we in elementary school? What's going on here?* She proceeded to tell me that this whole deal would fall apart if I didn't apologize and that I essentially needed to get down on my knees and beg for forgiveness. She also told me she was so scared of this guy that he was giving her diarrhea. Actual diarrhea. She was scared not only that we wouldn't close but also of what *else* he might do to us. It was all hysterical and absurd. So then I had to deal with her diarrhea and beg on hands and knees . . . not my specialty.

Of course, knowing how upset he was, I called him, and he answered. I said, "Listen, I know we had some back-

and-forth dialogue and I threw out the word 'stupid' loosely. I don't feel that way about you, and I'm sorry I offended you." And it was over. What's funny about all of this is that, after this conversation, the deal got more complicated and his agent couldn't hack it, so we began dealing with him directly. We ended up creating a really close relationship with this guy. And after calling him stupid, almost losing the deal, and maybe having a hit out on me at one point or another . . . he's now my client.

When you take something too far, the only thing *not* to do is not do *anything*. Not calling would have been the wrong thing to do. You have to have some humility in life in general. But especially when you screw up (whether or not that was your intention), you have to own your own shit. I've never had a hard time apologizing. If I feel like something was misinterpreted, or I said something that I didn't mean, I'll own up to it. I'll acknowledge that I feel bad. Whether it's to a tough mobster or businessman or to one of my best friends, getting out in front of it without a lot of drama has always served me well. I call or shoot a text or send an email and tell someone what I think about how I screwed up. And I apologize. People love to forget, and when you take humor too far, which happens some-times, especially with that defensive humor, you've got to be prepared to own that.

HUMOR IS A HAPPY PLACE

Last summer I went on a trip with thirty gay men. I call them "my gays." Not only are they my favorite people to be around, but they are the fucking funniest people I know. You put those men in a room with me and I'm in my happy place. I'm totally crazy with them. It's a no-holds-barred, judgment-free zone and the most fun place to be because of it. Sometimes people need permission to be their wildest, funniest selves. These guys give that to me in spades. There's no part of myself I have to hide, and it's incredibly freeing.

Leading up to this trip, I was a bit nervous, because it was thirty men, all in relationships, and me. I called my friend Bradley—he's from Tennessee—and told him my concern about being a bit of the odd woman out. His response? "Precious girl, we are your audience. I don't think you fully understand, we are your *biggest* fans. So you're putting yourself out there. You're going to shine. And it's going to be fine." He wasn't wrong.

This trip we were on was a two-week vacation across a few different islands. One of our stops was in Mykonos. After a fun night at dinner, all the guys went home. I did not. I went out dancing with my sister Kristen, and let's just say I woke up the next morning next to a very cute and very young guy. With a roommate. My first waking thought was *I have got to get the hell out of here.* So I'm WhatsApping our concierge, Jorgos, telling him I need out, but I don't know the address of where I am, and I am clearly not waking the roommates. I'm sitting in the dark looking for anything that will give me a clue as to where they should come pick me up. I'm at some random guy's random villa on an island I got to just yesterday. Our concierge tells me to drop a pin and share my location. *How the hell do you share a location on WhatsApp?* So he sends me a YouTube video that I sit in the dark watching. We're going back and forth trying to orchestrate my departure from this ridiculous night where my judgment was mildly impaired. Don't judge. Finally he writes, "I'll text you when we're there and run out. Car will be there in five."

When I got into the car, I realized this whole entire back-and-forth had fifteen other people on the text chain. I arrived home to the boys waiting for me by the pool. My friend Diggy's first words to me were "I have been up in my kaftan smoking cigarettes like Mrs. Roper waiting for you to get home. I want every detail." They would accept nothing less than a minute-by-minute breakdown of everything that happened. They were beside themselves and made me take a "slut lap" around the lunch table. They couldn't have been happier about the whole ridiculous night. There was *no* shame. In fact, there was nothing but roaring laughter.

I love these men because they allow me to be 100 percent authentic to myself. It reminds me to live in a very light and humorous way where you can poke fun, make no apologies, and celebrate what makes us all unique and different. It's just a safe place to be—a place where people are genuine. It makes you pretty fucking free, and honestly they're my favorite people to travel with. Being with people who find the funny in everything helps you be more funny, honestly.

They also help you to choose not to take yourself too seriously. Because look, there are so many big things that will happen in any of our lives that we need to choose to live with humor (and with other people who find life humorous). It's a much better place to be. Shortly after this Greece foray, I was at a girlfriend's birthday party where a bunch of the women were divorced. I met this girl who had gone through a situation very similar to the one I had (of course, also in Mykonos—shocker), and she was a total hoot. She asked if I met anyone on my trip, and I said, "Well, I wouldn't say I *met* him," and proceeded to tell her the ridiculous story. She couldn't believe I'd told her that whole thing and proceeded to tell me *her* story, which was worse than mine. We were both cracking up, thinking how it was fucking brilliant and how we had to go out. Meanwhile there were a few other women at this party in similar situations—recently divorced walking around with a gray cloud over their heads. And I thought to myself, *You can live like that, or you can have a fun night and an ahemmm-year-old in Greece and laugh about it.* You choose. I know which route I'm choosing, and I don't need to drop a pin to find it.

Laughing really is the best medicine for anything going on in our lives. And if you can be around people like that, who treat humor as a celebration of life, it'll make you feel the same way—and remind you to do the same for others. Life is a complicated roller coaster of emotions. Up-and-down shit happens to you. I'm certainly not going to spend it so seriously, feeling bad about myself. I've been there and done that before. But at some point you make a choice to be hopeful and happy and *live.* Humor does that. As do funny people.

HAND OVER THE TORCH

You don't always get to be the one with the punch line. Sometimes you have to hand the torch over and let someone else be funny. If you do this well, it'll end in the same results: everyone lightens up and everyone wins.

My friend and costar Josh Flagg is eccentric and hilarious and the type of person you have to hand the torch to. The best way to have fun with Josh is to live in that world;

otherwise you're going to be outside the circle. And it means handing over the torch and letting his humor lead, which, as you can imagine, is not easy for me as someone who considers myself pretty fucking funny.

This summer Flagg asked me to be a guest on his YouTube show, *Herr Flegenheimer*, which is a parody where he plays a German man who looks an awful lot like him, but with a mustache and a terrible accent. When he asked me to be in this skit, I had no idea what I was getting myself into. But I know Flagg, and I knew it was going to be hysterical. I had a choice, though, to have fun with it or to think it was completely ridiculous (it was). At one point in the skit we were kissing at the dinner table. I think he slipped a little tongue.

When you let go and let someone drive you around playing ten different kinds of farts on the Tesla speakers (he did that), it's quite freeing. When you've got two entertainers in the room, like you had with me and Flagg, and two people who want to be successful, someone has to relinquish control to the other. People who can make life fun and exciting with their humor build yours. But you have to go with the flow and let them take the lead. You don't always have to be the funniest person in the room. Sometimes you can just be the person laughing. And with Flagg I'm always laughing.

You get to choose when to be that person, instead of the

one entertaining. Often, one of the most powerful things you can do is to shine that warmth of attention on someone else and let them feel the spotlight. For instance, if you're tag-teaming on a pitch with someone and it's clear their brand of humor is hitting home—let it hit home. If you're at a lunch meeting with someone who has incredibly funny stories to tell from the weekend, let them break the ice with their stories instead of trying to insert your own. That's part of controlling the room: you don't always have to be the center of every conversation and joke. I love giving that attention to someone else and letting them shine. I'm still in control. I'm making the conscious choice to live in someone else's space. It shows how confident you are when you're willing to hand the attention over. When they recognize that you're a strong female with confidence, they're going to be magnetized. They'll have already assumed you were going to own that room. But they'll also probably have assumed that it was *going to be all about you.* Instead you're saying, *Come into my world. Come on over. Let me show you how great this can be. And once you've met me and understand who I am, let me turn it over to you and make you feel really important.*

It's so easy to do. Ask them a ton of questions. Ask follow-up questions to show you're really listening. Show you're intrigued by what they're saying. And they'll walk away feeling really special.

Whether you're giving someone else the stage or stepping up yourself, try when you can to find the humor. Go to a comedy club and learn to laugh. Figure out what makes you smile, and smile at that. Take improv. And for fuck's sake, find a way to not take yourself so seriously. You don't have to be the funniest person in the room, because I don't know if funny can *actually* be taught, but you can be taught to lighten up. And loosen up. Not everyone is going to be hilarious, but everyone can find the humor in things. And you should whenever possible.

Chapter 6

DRESS FOR AN EDGE

*D*ressing the part matters, especially if you want to achieve the right outcomes. There's a reason you don't wear sequins during the day. Just like you shouldn't wear a low-cut dress and expect to win the business of a newly married couple (I mean, unless they're swingers, which we can save for another chapter). In reality, you can do whatever you want, but it's probably not smart. When people judge whether or not they trust your ability to represent their interests, one of the things they consider is how you put yourself together. That's been true for all of human history. Luckily, this is all in your control. You can have an edge on your competition by sub-liminally letting the person in the room know that you fully understand (without even trying) where you're at and that you are the right one for the job. They'll think: *She* *knows her audience and how to appeal to that audience. She's definitely got this.* Which you do. So let's show them that.

Whenever I need to feel 100 percent like *I've got this*, I wear red. It's been my kill color since I was in high school. I've always felt good in it. For my first homecoming dance, when my mom took me shopping for a dress, I came out of the dressing room in this (now god-awful but then ahhhmazing) red satin ruched dress that had puffy sleeves and was off the shoulder; totally my jam. It really took the attention away from the bizarro spiral perm that I'd insisted on getting—and my mom couldn't talk me out of. Despite the distracting perm, my mom couldn't wipe the *wow* look off her face. "Red is your color," she said.

Fast-forward to this past year, and I've just been named the global ambassador for the Royal Atlantis, which is a world-renowned development in the United Arab Emirates. This is an extraordinary property and currently the largest in Dubai. Between the architects, designers, money, and construction, the sheer star power of this team is like nothing I've ever seen. When my company's international real estate partner was looking for a U.S. connection for this Royal Atlantis residence, they chose me. It was an enormous honor to be attached to this type of luxury brand. My job as an ambassador would be to educate brokers and buyers alike that the Atlantis is a place for their clients to invest money in secondary or primary residences. But to lock in this partnership, I needed to go to Dubai first and meet the man in charge.

Which means that I'd be walking into the office of one of the biggest developers in the world. I had to show him I was the person for the job, and I was representing my entire agency. This had to go well. While I'd never been to Dubai, I was well versed in the historically conservative norms for women in the UAE. This man I was meeting with was powerful beyond measure and had a reputation for being very attached to royalty. He was a big deal, and I was totally out of my comfort zone. I was a fucking wreck, terrified, and to top it off I had no idea what to wear to this meeting. I wanted to respect the culture, but I still wanted to feel like me. I was very concerned about how I'd be perceived. I wanted to dress right and appropriately, but I wanted to embrace my own identity at the same time. So I did a lot of homework leading up to the meeting.

I had a lot of questions for the liaison who walked me through what was about to happen—which was that I would be introduced to him, and he'd be in his traditional all-white garb. I asked if I was allowed to shake his hand and if they had any suggestions on best practices for meeting attire. They instructed me to have my shoulders covered and to dress appropriately. So I chose to wear a red dress that, looking back, was pretty bold given the situation, but it still fell well within the boundaries of everything I'd learned about the region and doing business there.

The meeting ended up being an incredible success. He was a charming man, so lovely and kind. The type of confident person who wasn't trying to prove anything. Remember the personality types? He was definitely a team player. He showed such curiosity about me and my experience as someone visiting. This was a person who was very clearly in the pole position but made me feel very comfortable and eager to show him what I had. Red dress and all.

There are so many factors that go into doing this—dressing for an edge—right. It's as externally driven as it is internal. You've got to know the dynamics of the room you're walking into so you know how to dress for it. But you also have to know your own internal barometer of what makes you comfortable and what helps you feel like you're showing up as your most powerful self. It all communicates a level of confidence that's unspoken but loud . . . and it's not one-fashion-advice-fits-all for every person, situation, or intended outcome. Look, dressing the part won't be the reason you win, but it will give you an edge.

BEFORE YOU DRESS

You've got to know what makes you feel good, or dressing for an edge is a moot point. But that can be hard, because people have opinions about what you should and shouldn't do. I know *a lot* about dealing with all that noise. As someone who's on a TV show, my wardrobe choices not only get seen by millions of people but, in the past, have been controlled by someone other than me. Let me tell you, I've never felt worse than when I was trying to cater to every whim of someone's opinion on what I should wear. Being on TV for the first time, I did this constantly. I let people's opinions on my blouse color, my hairstyle, and my outfit choices get me all worked up. I took advice on my appearance when I shouldn't have. And I let all the noise about "looking the part" get under my skin. My ability to be in the moment suffered because of it.

I've learned that it's essential to wear what you feel good in. When someone fusses with you too much and then you don't feel like yourself, your best work can't come forward. It's the same as if you try to wear something trendy but you don't actually feel good in it. Don't wear it, then. If you can't feel sexy, in control, and powerful in everything you put on, take it off.

Looking back with that in mind, I should have confronted

all of the advice that I was getting. I should have told myself, *You're aiming for authenticity, so show up and dress in a way that allows you to deliver that. I'm a real estate agent. I'm not a patent attorney. I've got to feel like me.*

You have control over this situation. You need to position yourself to be in rooms that allow you to dress in ways that make you feel like *you* while adhering to the general best practices of the culture, room, and audience that you're catering to. Whether you're looking to Instagram, magazines, or runways for inspiration, ultimately you have to be in your own comfort zone. If you can't hold yourself in a way that makes you feel comfortable, then the entire look has to go. If the only thing people see is your inability to be comfortable in your own skin, that's when your outfit wears you, and you don't wear your outfit.

THE (NO DRESS CODE) DRESS CODE

I can't tell you exactly what to wear. Most situations won't be that straightforward. Even if there's a general dress code for an office, an event, or a function, it's up to you to decide how to operate within those "rules" so that you feel good doing you. This can be harder in certain situations than in others. Which is why whenever you're getting dressed, once you know what works and makes *you* feel great, you're ready to assess what would be best for the room or situation. There are a few questions you should ask yourself before you pick out what exactly you'll be wearing, especially if something important is on the line:

1. *Who's* going to be in the room?
2. *Where* are we meeting?
3. *What* are we meeting about?
4. *How* do I want them to perceive me?

The Who: There's always a chance you're not going to know your audience as well as you want to, so you've got to be comfortable in whatever it is that you're wearing. And how you hold yourself is a huge part of that. You've got to dress for who you're with but still retain your identity. There are a lot of ways to answer *who* someone is. Taking the time to understand and evaluate what type of person they are will help you choose what version of yourself to be: creative? edgy? buttoned up? casual? trendy?

I pay the most attention to *ages* and *industries* when I'm considering what's the right thing to wear. Recently I had a listing appointment with the Altman brothers. I wanted to be respectful of them and also cognizant of the fact that I was meeting with a former mayor—the last Republican mayor this city had and someone who came from a completely different time, generationally speaking. So I read up on him and ultimately decided to dress in more neutral colors, with a camel-colored pencil skirt, black pumps, a shirt, and not a lot of jewelry. I looked good, but it wasn't too much. I'm always going to be cautious like this when I'm in an environment with someone who has far more life experience and is of a different time period altogether. A meeting with a ninety-year-old conservative ex-mayor isn't the place to take fashion risks and throw down a little edge. On the other hand, I'll take many more chances when I'm meeting with younger generations, primarily because I'm older than they are, so I'm more confident. Funny how age does that.

I also pay attention to someone's industry, like are they corporate or creative? If I'm meeting with someone in a creative field, I'm more inclined to be creative myself. Granted, I'm living in one of the most liberal cities in the United States, so I work with a lot of people who work in a creative field and are successful at it. That's made it easy to know how to dress with that creative edge. A while back, I sat down with an art collector covered in tats who had a vintage T-shirt line he'd sold for a bunch of money and just reeked of cool. I would have felt like a jackass if I had worn what I did to the meeting with the former mayor. Instead, the art collector's edgy sense of style allowed me to explore that, too. He's comfortable in his version of cool and was comfortable with mine. Here in LA we get to own our individuality through fashion, but it's not always like that, which is why you've gotta keep asking yourself who it is you're trying to get on equal footing with, which starts with how you show up.

In my opinion, you should always mirror who you're meeting with as best you can. If you don't have the ability to gain any information on someone before meeting with them (it happens!), always go for the middle ground. Pick something nondescript but well tailored that will allow you to blend in to any situation. Be offensive to no one. Think nice fabrics, basic colors, and true to you. But if you have information on someone, mirror them always.

This is probably a good time to remind you that when you're evaluating *who* you're meeting with, it's worth considering their gender. There are people who might not agree with me on this, but how you dress for men is different from how you dress for women. I'm not going to wear a tight pencil skirt and a tucked-in V-neck blouse or a slim-fitting dress that shows my curves if I'm meeting with a couple. I like feeling sexy, feminine, and powerful *for myself* when I walk into a room, but I also like keeping a feminine connection when I meet with a couple. Number one, it's who I am—I am just a girl's girl—and number two, I know most men ("most" being the operative word, before y'all get offended), and I am not going to allow what is in my control (my outfit) to potentially engage male attention in the wrong way. I wish this were different, but it just isn't. Human nature. It's worth keeping factors like these in mind. Similar to age, you want to understand the dynamic between the people in the room. Maybe your client is a super chic, boundary-pushing woman but her business partner is a conservative old guy. You've got to dress for the lowest common conservative denominator. Wear the thing that will please both of them. Because there *is* such a thing as too much. When you wear a tight, form-fitting skirt, it can get too sexy fast. There's a fine line where something goes from well-fitting and form-fitting to too snug. This also depends on your body type. One woman can wear a dress and look totally professional, but if someone else puts it on, it becomes completely inappropriate for a business meeting. You have to know your body.

Remember, when you're evaluating the *who*, no matter who you're meeting and how much or how little you know, you know *something*. So dress for that.

The Where: Once you know who you're meeting with, you've got to take into consideration *where* you're meeting. You could be meeting with the exact same person in two different locations, and you'd need to make completely different choices. This just happened to me recently with meetings with my developer client. When I first met with this developer, I'd done so at his office. So I wore a pencil skirt, pumps, and a blouse (which is one of my favorite go-to outfits). However, once he awarded me the listing, I was meeting with him on a construction site. If I'd shown up in the same style of outfit I had before, I'd have looked like an idiot and probably lost his trust in my understanding of where these properties were at. This is a client who lives in Malibu, who works in Malibu, and whose life is in Malibu. If you've never been, let's just say this is a place that's overwhelmingly relaxed and peaceful. It differs from any other place in the world, and this person was building to that type of serenity. His whole vision was to be designed with the Malibu ethos in mind. I needed to show that I understood that.

At this particular on-site meeting, I was going to meet with him, his wife, and photographers to take photos of the properties. If I put on the red dress that I'd worn in Dubai, I'd look like an asshole. If I wore what I had to our first meeting, I'd also look like an asshole. So I put on a pair of button-fly jeans and a sweatshirt and carried my kelly-green Birkin bag. And I fit right in. His kid even commented on my purse and said, "Dad, did you see it? I want one." To which he basically said, *Good luck.* Even though I was completely dressed down and far less "professional" than I had been when first meeting the biggest client I've ever had, I still had that piece (my Birkin bag) that made me feel confident enough to be in jeans and a sweatshirt on the job. I not only knew *who* I was meeting with but understood the full context of *where* we were meeting. I had already gotten the job. I didn't need to show up as a polished saleswoman. I needed to show I understood where my client was at and what the task was: photography. I simply couldn't have worn this if we were meeting downtown or in Beverly Hills.

The What: You've got to know your intended outcome for any meeting or situation, because that'll affect how you choose to dress. When I'm working at the office and jamming with my team, you'll find me in ripped jeans, a T-shirt, and some edgy jewelry, because I'm not trying to win anything; I'm just trying to get my work done.

But if I'm selling—in a pitch or a listing presentation or an in-person negotiation—you better believe I'm dressed. Because I want to win that business, I'm going to look like I'm someone they can trust to do just that. It's similar to why I wore a pencil skirt for the initial meeting that led to pitching for the biggest listing of my career but then showed up in jeans once the work started—because I didn't need to win anything; I needed to do the work. I've made this mistake before when I've shown up overdressed to a job site, looking like an idiot because I was in four-inch heels at a construction site with no foundation to walk on. I probably didn't need to do that. I wasn't selling; I was working. So know *what* you're there to do and it'll help inform *what* you choose to wear.

The How: You've got to put yourself in the other person's position and ask yourself how you'd like them to perceive you. Do you want them to think you can handle this job? Their business? Do you want them to feel like you're approachable? Maybe you want them to think of you as always coloring within the lines? Or maybe as a statement maker instead?

If I want to be perceived as powerful, I'm wearing a dress and generally a strong color, like red, with a very high stiletto. If I want to be perceived as approachable, I'm going with jeans, a sweater, and a nice tennis shoe. If I want to be perceived as attentive, I'll take out my multiple piercings and go with simple studs, black pants, and a pump.

When I went in to pitch that huge listing, I wanted the whole team to perceive me as someone who could handle this level of business and play at the height of this real estate game. So I came dressed like it. I wore a black dress that had long sleeves and a plunging neckline that I covered with a camisole so it wasn't inappropriate. I had to look like *the woman who can handle it.* I was going to be representing a $100 million property, so I wanted them to see me as sophisticated, as someone who could not only sell one of the homes but own one of them. It's all a perception game, but one you have to be willing to play. It doesn't require much more than asking yourself what you'd like them to think and then dressing accordingly. If you're not sure what your outfit says, snap a text to an honest girl-friend. She'll tell you. If you want something, you've got to look like you want it.

THE BASICS

I don't care how much money you make or what your background is, trying to live up to and live within the standards set for women has gotten out of control. Wearing the right shoes, skirt, bag, and top has moved beyond aspiration; it's become expected. And it's totally unattainable. But it doesn't have to be (nor should it be).

Even as a very successful woman, I totally used to feel this. I couldn't attain the norm that was set for me to wear, buy, and look like. I was ordering a ton of shit online with the intention of returning it. But then you lose track of what you're actually returning. Before you know it, you have an out-of-control credit card bill and a bunch of items that won't be relevant in six months, and what do you have to show for it?

You have to pick and choose the pieces that are most important to you: the ones that will always be classic. As someone who loves fashion, that's a niche I've found to be really interesting. Which item of clothing is worth more of an investment? And which piece is trendy and thus irrelevant in a few months? These are the items that I think are the most important to have dialed in, that can stay in your closet for years instead of months (and that are worth spending more on if you want). Pieces are great because you'll have them in your closet forever to mix and match. But this really comes down to knowing which pieces are *your* pieces based on what looks good on you:

- *A **well-designed, awesome-fitting skirt.*** You'll be able to wear this for the next eight years instead of just next season.
- ***Men's-cut tailored, white shirt.*** It goes with everything and can be totally elevated with accessories. Note: you should buy a new one every year.
- ***High-waisted denim*** to dress up or dress down.
- *A **really well-cut dress.*** Figure out what's best for your body and buy this in a simple color so that you can have it in your closet forever.
- *A **little black dress.*** Find something appropriate for your neckline and body type.
- ***Track pants,*** which can be sporty but still sophisticated.
- ***Black blazer with a twist,*** so you can look pulled together in an instant.
- ***Great, classic, designer pumps.*** No kitten heels, please. Get a couple of colors.

Whatever pieces you go with, it's worth investing in higher-quality versions that fit you well. Don't underestimate the power of a good tailor to take a piece off the rack and make it look like it was custom made for you. Consider which piece can be your signature look and which color can be you signature color. Anything can be a signature look, as long as you feel good in it, it's versatile, and you rock the piece well. Erika on my team, for example, always wears color and patterns. It's her thing, and she changes it depending on the situation. The brighter the better, and it totally works for her. It absolutely suits her personality and instantly makes her more approachable. My former business partner always wore jeans, riding boots, a blazer, and a hat. The jeans color would change depending on the season. It was very equestrian and regal and totally worked without looking over-the-top or like she was trying too hard. I have a male agent friend who legitimately just wears black T-shirts or button-downs and black jeans every single day. It works for him. It's simple but elegant and has the right amount of edge.

If red is my color, skirts are my signature piece. Here are my five favorite ways to wear them, which make them suitable for almost any room I'm walking into:

1. ***Skirt and blouse.*** Paired with some heels and jewelry, it's perfect for any meeting.

2. *Skirt and T-shirt.* This dresses it down and looks great no matter where you're going.

3. *Skirt and boyfriend sweater.* This looks edgy and fun and can be playful and approachable when you need to be.

4. *Skirt and man's shirt.* It evokes an eighties sort of career woman with an edge. This is great situations where you want to look cool and professional.

5. *Shorter skirt with men's blazer.* This gives that menswear vibe again, but with a peek of femininity. The skirt shouldn't hit any higher than a few inches above the knee.

If you're trying to find your signature piece, take photos of yourself to see with more distance whether the lines flatter. That's pretty much the bottom line. If I look at photos of myself in floral, I appear to be three times larger than I actually am. And the drapey-fabric, feminine dresses that I so desperately want to look good in just add inches to an already curvy physique. Be honest about how something looks on you, and decide if that's a look you'll continue iterating. I'll have entire seasons when I don't buy anything new and will just get a new basic or a new twist on one of my favorites. That's what will keep you modern without having to completely change what works best on you.

Speaking of season, your body might change year to year. I mean, we're women! Whether you're working out more or less, feeling stressed, or are pregnant or postpartum, take time to evaluate if something was working last year but maybe isn't the right fit this year. If it doesn't fit you right and wearing it brings you anything but strong positive feelings, skip it. If you're feeling bloated that day from a weekend of margaritas and tortilla chips, don't wear it. Wear whatever makes you feel good in your skin at that moment, which, as we all know, changes day to day and year to year.

HIGH AND LOW

Once you have the classic pieces that you love, you can start pairing them with trends that *aren't* worth investing in. I've tried to keep up with trends (like, oh god, that floral look), and I end up looking like two-ton Annie (my mom used to say that all the time and it stuck; I wish it didn't) in them. It's simply too much fabric for me. I look better in something more tailored. This is just how trends operate—some trends are great for some people and very much not for others. Cut to *why they are trends and not classics.*

When you want to play with trends but don't want to

blow your wallet, houses like Zara, H&M, Revolve, and Topshop do this well. They specialize in taking the high-end versions of fashions and re-creating them at lower-end price points that are great for one season. Maybe you want that cutout top, but it's probably not going to resonate with you next year? Snag it from one of these places. I match Zara tops with an expensive skirt and pumps all the time. Plus, how much different does it all look? With amazing price points from these places, you can pull off all the expensive looks for less than $100. Anything that's made really well and is expensive is going to be copied and thus affordable.

While we're on the topic of *expensive*, let me remind you that more money doesn't equal more style. I've seen some really rich people with terrible taste, which typically looks like being an overboard brand whore. It makes you look cheap if you're wearing a Gucci T-shirt with a Chanel belt and a diamond-encrusted Rolex. It's too much and reeks of trying too hard. You don't have to do that in order to look good. You don't have to be rich at all in order to look fully polished. That's the beauty of fashion today.

If you're not sure how to mix high and low, like expensive pieces with cheap trends, look to Instagram and fashion bloggers. They have followers all over the country, so most of it isn't city-specific fashion. They might have super aspirational pictures, but their tips and finds are very accessible. They mix pieces well and make fashion more accessible than it was when I was growing up and all you had was high-fashion magazines. Before, you didn't know what someone was wearing. No one would brag about their top being $39. Now everyone has that access, so there's really no excuse not to be able to create looks if you want to. Even if you have no ability to "invest" high dollar amounts in pieces, you can figure out through these fashion influencers which brands will make you look great and pulled together and on trend without spending obscenely.

While you're figuring out what's best for you at your price point and for your body shape, don't forget about accessorizing. Being on trend with your jewelry is a major piece of elevating a simple jeans-and-T-shirt look. You could be in a crisp, white T-shirt and jeans you feel good in and throw on a cool necklace that's on trend and a great, colorful bag, and all of a sudden you look incredible and pulled together.

There's a bunch of great accessory-rental companies, too, if you're into that sort of thing. You could rent a killer bag for a few months, or even a very expensive watch or your entire closet, and no one would be the wiser. I've done this with watches because they're really expensive but I get tired of wearing the same one every day. These rental companies allow you to switch up your look and make it completely affordable while you do.

Remember, fashion prides itself on what's trendy, what's within the rules and what's not, and what's in season. But the only rule you actually need to follow is dressing for what makes you feel completely capable of owning every room you're in. You don't have to spend all kinds of money and/or take anyone's advice other than your own. If you keep in mind that every room and situation is different, you'll navigate this gracefully. Ask yourself *who* you're meeting with, *what* you're meeting about, *where* you're meeting, and *how* you want to be perceived, and you'll be able to make choices that result in a successful outcome. What you're wearing is never the most important thing, but the optics can either magnify your capabilities or detract from them. It's worth it to consider what makes you feel unstoppable, so that what you're wearing gives you exactly the edge you need.

Chapter 7

....

SELF-AWARENESS
IS A MUST

W ant a fast track to self-awareness? Try putting yourself on a television show for millions to see. To date, my decision to be on *Million Dollar Listing Los Angeles* was the biggest choice I've ever made, because it would really represent my truth. Good, bad, perfect, or ugly—people were going to judge me, my marriage, my motherhood, my work, and my social life. I was self-aware enough to know all of that, but also to know that I'm at a time in my life where I'm less affected by how people perceive me. I was *finally* ready to put myself in that position. I was finally ready to unapologetically live my own life. The show became a mirror, one that showed both me and the world that I was 1,000 percent good with me— so much so that I was willing to put myself on TV. There was nothing about me (or my flaws) that I didn't already have a handle on. For example, I can be super defensive, which is weird to watch even if you know it about yourself. I can be a little too fast and overzealous, which turns people off. I tell bad jokes, and sometimes I say something offensive in the spirit of being funny, but it's not funny. However, I know these things about myself, which makes seeing them on camera somewhat less painful. I decided that I was going to live my life the way I was going to live it, whether there's a camera in front of me or not.

Believe it or not, it feels good to be imperfect. When you announce that, and walk away from this obsession with perfection, it humanizes you. There's nothing worse than walking around expecting perfection and then inevitably screwing it up. You're just a flawed version of perfection when you do that. It causes so much anxiety that you can't live normally. You'll hit a wall eventually. People *will* figure it out. You're so much better off owning your imperfections. If you announce and recognize you're absolutely *not* perfect and don't need to be, then you have so much more space to run and be brilliant. It'll feel so much better to let it go and not have to carry that burden of perfection anymore. You're not going to be great at everything. No one is.

However, to live without the fear of imperfection and instead make choices for you, you've got to be unapologetic about your decisions and at peace with your weaknesses. Whether you fall on your face or not, it's *your* life and *your* choices. If you're afraid to dig in and refuse to learn about yourself, you'll never be living a truly free and honest life. You'll be living one that you hope fits. That you hope succeeds. But that's the surest way to be immobilized by fear.

There's nothing more valuable than someone who owns their faults. To be self-aware, especially in business, you've got to understand your weaknesses and be able to talk about them. There's real power in that, because it shows that you're confident. When you can simply talk about a mistake that you made and talk about how you grew from correcting that in whatever facet of your life, you'll win. Women are often scared to show their weaknesses, but we've got to own them in order to own the room. You can't become more successful if you can't figure out what you did wrong.

I've made plenty of bad decisions and handled choices I made with less grace than I could have. And I've had more situations go sideways in both my business and my life than I can count. I don't think any have felt more excruciating than a scene that was caught on camera in my first season on *Million Dollar Listing Los Angeles*. It was sort of my greatest fear coming true, but when your flaws *are* actually out there for the world to see, you learn just how strong you are. The only way to learn that strength is in the fire of getting to know your failures and your weaknesses up close and personal. For me that time came when it appeared that I didn't know what grade my daughter was in. I knew exactly what grade she was in, I assure you, but it looked like I didn't for a number of reasons, one of which was that I second-guessed myself. I second-guessed myself on camera that day because my husband was not happy that I decided to do the show and pitted family and my work against each other. Was I spending too much time in one area and not the other? Well, I allowed that insecurity to get used against me, and it blew up in my face.

See, my then-husband, Jason, didn't want me to do the show. I took the opportunity anyway, which sounds selfish, right? I'm sure. But it was a much more thoughtful decision that I thank god every day that I made. But back to this particular moment. We were shooting our first-ever scene together, and it was supposed to be easy breezy. We were meeting for lunch and assumed we would chat about the kids and what was happening at work. I could tell he was nervous. I was nervous, too. This was only the fourth or fifth time I had even been on camera. So we threw around some stuff about work and then started talking about our daughters, beginning with my oldest, Juliet. We discussed how she was doing really great and coming into her own and how proud I was of her. Jason followed that by saying, "Scarlett, on the other hand . . ." and I responded with "We'll see. She's only in the second grade."

He point-blank looked at me and just coldly said, "Our daughter's in third." To which I replied, "No, she's not. . . . Wait, yes, she is. . . . No, she's not." I thought to correct him yet again, but then he was so confident, brazen, and condescending. It was really awful, looking back. I just watched it again when I was writing this chapter, and it still cuts deep. But in that moment, sitting across from him, I just kind of froze, because he was *so* certain that I thought, *God, wait a minute. Am I crazy? Do I have her grade wrong?* He then looked at me with such disgust in his eyes and said, "Work much?" And I just fell apart right there in the scene. I thought in that small moment that I was a horrible mother who had forgotten what grade her daughter was in.

I know my daughter's grade. I knew it then. My husband was totally gaslighting me on camera. You know when you are debating a topic with someone, and the other person is *so* confident in their comment that you think, *Well, maybe that did happen. . . . Maybe I did say that. . . . Maybe I am wrong?* That's what Jason did to me. I was so humiliated.

After we cut cameras, I told Jason, "You recognize you were the one in the wrong here. It was such a dick move. And I'm going to defend myself in my next interview." I knew that if I didn't speak the truth, I would be perceived as a terrible mother, a work-obsessed asshole who didn't care about her kids. I did discuss it briefly in an interview following that scene where I cleared up my side of that story. Unfortunately, that interview didn't air until a week later. So in the time between those episodes, I was bullied on every social-media platform, with people saying I was "a shit mother and wife" and declaring, "Jason should leave her" and "She cares too much about work to care about her kids." It was awful, but I came out the other side stronger.

I returned next season with an even firmer sense of self, despite that now I also have an ex-husband, and our kids do not appear on the show. The reality of that family decision creates a strong visual on television for the viewer. Life happens, and the conversation we had on camera plus the choice we made for them to not be a part of the show the following year again confirms this tough-girl persona where all I care about is work and partying with my friends. People who watch view me in this certain way—like some tough chick who never sees her girls and who doesn't care about anything remotely personal. But this is where self-awareness plays its most important role: I know who I am. I know that I'm not made of steel. I know that I'm soft and vulnerable and full of feelings. I also know that I'm a passionate mother who has a tendency to second-guess myself, which allows me to better manage it. I know that I've left meetings and gotten into my car just before the tears came streaming down my face. The world might think I'm a hard-ass, but I know who I truly am. That's why when you can own it all—misperception on TV, making mistakes, having faults, second-guessing yourself—there's not much that will stop you . . . imperfections and all.

MY WEAKNESSES ARE MANY

I'll be the first to admit that I get things wrong (not my kid's grade in school, though). And that I'm terrible at things. But if you know what you hate doing and you know what you love, you can optimize your choices for the latter over time. Every strength has its trade-off, and vice versa. What matters is that you can see how a strength could be manipulated, too.

EVERY STRENGTH HAS ITS SHADOW

If you're great at connecting . . . you may get overly in tune with someone else's needs over your own.

If you're super confident . . . you may seem intimidating to some.

If you're a big-picture thinker . . . you might have a hard time with the details.

If you're detail oriented . . . you may not see the long-term plan.

If you're great at strategy . . . you might always be thinking too many steps ahead.

If you're super organized . . . you might have a hard time with blue-sky thinking.

If you're a good listener . . . you may have a hard time asserting your opinion.

If you make quick decisions . . . you may miss something.

If you're a great negotiator . . . you may be viewed as tough to deal with.

If you're persuasive . . . you might have people back out on you later.

If you're systems oriented . . . you might not be as creative.

We all have to face these trade-offs. In my life and my business, I'm so macro about everything. Even in being organized, I'm macro! That's how macro I am, which I know is a massive contradiction. Overall, I want things to be a certain way, but my follow-through is not great. This has only really come up recently as my team has grown. There are more people to manage. There's more business. There are more personalities. The bigger and more successful I have become, the more complex my team has become—both at work and at home. I legit color-code my calendar. I have eight different colors for the various aspects of my life. I'm obsessive about the timing of my schedule. I love being able to look at one place on my calendar and know: *This is for the girls, this is appointments, this is work, this is show.* At home this is really easy to do because it's just me. But as I've been running a team and worrying about everyone else all the time, it's gotten a little bit crazy. I've gotten lost in it all, because I haven't set up systems that can help control my team at scale. Things are falling through the cracks. My major weakness is maintaining the level of structure I need with an entire team, so that it can function better and be more effective. Simple systems worked great as a solo operator. But with a team I need more complex systems than my talent and skills can manage.

There's more. I look like a marketing machine because my name and face are everywhere, but I actually hate marketing, even though I'm very visual. I'm aesthetically inclined in life in general, whether it's designing a house, picturing a room painted a certain color, or visualizing the way I want a photo to turn out. But without the skill set to do it, marketing really is the most time-consuming piece of my business, because design assets are needed everywhere in order to sell—mailers, letters, social media, different types of print collateral, billboards, magazines, email blasts, and websites. It's excruciating to have this marketing battle week after week for every property.

Well, when your areas of opportunity—like marketing needs and team needs—come together at once, you can end up in some pretty tough situations, like a valued member of your team about to have a meltdown.

I've failed my team a little bit, especially in the last few years as things have gotten incredibly busy. Weaknesses don't have to be a huge problem, if you can identify them early and create necessary solutions. I've taken too long to do this in my own business, and by not managing my team effectively or understanding they needed more systems and support, especially in marketing, I haven't set them up for success. Basically, my director of ops, Elanor, had to become a marketing person. And she was struggling. She was making mistakes. My partner, Gina, was coming down on her hard. Gina is a perfectionist and the micro to my macro. She was really hard on Elanor for every mistake, to the point that my sweet little twenty-six-year-old director of ops was sitting in the office crying. This was a young woman who was always so ready to learn, incredibly willing to work crazy hours to do so . . . and she was in tears. When it was brought to my attention—because she'd never cry in front of me—I said no way. Not on my watch. I'm a big believer in working really hard but enjoying yourself. We can only kill ourselves if we have a good time while we're doing it. But I had to take ownership: the reason this was all happening was because I had her doing a bunch of work that wasn't a part of her job description. That was happening because I didn't have the marketing person I needed in place. It wasn't Gina's fault either. I sat Elanor down and said, "Look, I recognize this is my problem, not yours. I need to hire someone to do the job that you've been doing the last six months."

Self-awareness isn't just knowing where your areas of opportunity might be—in skills, in talents, in slipups—but, more important, taking responsibility when there's fallout. I could have let Elanor flail, fired her, and acted like she was not performing. However, I knew that wasn't the case. Because I knew that her problem was the by-product of my own weaknesses coming together. I needed to invest and get the right team in place, which included a marketing person, so we could have the systems needed for everyone to excel. Myself included. It's best to be up front about your weaknesses. You always want to be in front of a weakness if you foresee that it's going to come up. Share your flaws—with your team, a partner, or a client—and share what that solution might be. For example, with my team, I'm honest that I'm not a systems person, so I engage them about my solutions and about their ideas for solutions. I don't have to pretend to be outstanding at everything.

Easier said than done, of course. Accountability to yourself, first, is key. For the large majority of my career I couldn't just "hire what I wasn't good at." So if you're in that spot right now, it's not a problem. I can barely afford to hire for these things that I'm not good at, even with a business as big as mine. It requires taking a major financial hit, because that used to be money directly in my pocket. But as I've mentioned before, I'm confident it's what's needed to scale. However, during the earlier parts of my career, I did what needed to be done and tried to make it easy on myself while I did . . . even if I was terrible at what was required of me.

For example, contracts are a huge part of the real estate business. And while I know how to write a contract, my strengths are in personal relationships and understanding what makes someone tick. I'm best at getting someone from a "no" to a "yes." I'm not best when sitting behind a computer shoulder deep in contracts and navigating addendums. So I recognized that contracts were taking too much time, and I created a solution to compensate for this weakness.

California has a lot of frivolous lawsuits, and real estate can be particularly litigious. But when I first started in the business, I knew that legal and contracts would never be my strong suit. So I would keep copies of any legal language written by lawyers from deals, and I would reuse and restructure them to suit the deal I was on. I had a Dropbox folder called "Legal," and it was full of forms approved by attorneys, or written by attorneys, that I had kept over the years and cut and pasted into contracts more times than I can count. I recognized that I don't have the skill set for real estate law, nor am I passionate about it, but it's the expectation of our clients that we can explain it. I can't tell you how many times I had to sit and draft language that I was never comfortable with in the first place, but it was a part of my job. So I spent a ton of time on research, calling friends who were attorneys, asking for favors, and just gritting my teeth to find a way to get it done.

That's the beauty of knowing yourself, though. You know that just because something is taking a lot of brain power, and you might hate doing it or be terrible at it, doesn't mean *you* are terrible. It doesn't mean you should quit your job. It simply means that it's a part of your skill set that doesn't bring you pleasure. It really comes down to that—knowing what feels good. And what doesn't. When you can distinguish between the two, you can make more informed choices. And you can stop being so damn hard on yourself for not being perfect at everything. For a while, it just means you'll put in extra work around what doesn't feel good. Then, eventually, you'll have paid your dues or make different future choices accordingly, and you won't have to do as much of that anymore. It's about accountability to yourself, first and foremost. Knowing where you might need help can help get you that help.

INFORMED CHOICES

Most weaknesses can improve, even if they don't totally disappear. Here are some extra steps you can take to help solve for some of yours:

- Second-guessing your negotiation skills? Do a mock negotiation with a friend in law or sales (they basically negotiate for a living).

- If grammar just isn't your thing, download Grammarly so it catches any of your writing mistakes.

- If you're bad at presenting, buy a colleague an enormous coffee in exchange for listening to your dry run. (Make sure you try it without notes!)

- Feeling low on confidence? Call or email someone who loves you and ask them what you excel at.

- If you're nervous about sounding unintelligent at an upcoming social gathering, spend some time reading about what's happening in the world instead of scrolling through the 'gram.

TELL YOUR MANAGER WHAT YOU'RE BAD AT (YES, REALLY)

Earlier this year, I was having lunch with the West Coast president of Douglas Elliman, the company I work for. I told Stephen that I'm honestly struggling with this whole team thing. I'm so used to being a one-woman show, and I don't know how to get my team to perform at the level I need them performing at. If I'm going to grow this team to more than me and an assistant, I have to play at a different level. And I'm just not sure how to do that. He told me about an executive coach he and some other staff members were working with at Elliman, someone they really liked. He thought it would benefit me, and this is a man who knows me well enough that I was able to be honest about my struggles, and he could be honest about what might help. He knows I'm pulled in twenty-five different directions at all times, so if this was going to work, it needed to work. He offered to pay for six months of working with Aaron, the coach.

Sure enough, Aaron has helped me get some systems in place. See, I'd never had lead-generation and marketing systems in place before. I used Dropbox to manage my business with my assistant in order to stay on top of things. Once you have more than three or four people, though, that one-woman system is not set up for success. Spreadsheets and task-management platforms are not my cup of tea. I studied theater, for god's sake. There's not a universe where putting together marketing systems and lead-generation systems is going to be exciting for me. I'm completely oblivious to all of that.

Having this coach has been absolutely beneficial, particularly to my younger agents, Erika and Rob. I've always seen them as my young little babies who I needed to do everything for. As far as I was concerned, they were still my baby birds that I brought food home for as much as I could. In reality, they needed to function without me. But that's hard for them to do on their own without my putting these systems into place. Aaron forced me to finally do that, and he makes everyone, including me, accountable each and every week. I'm even forced to perform. What's amazing about having forced accountability is that it's really taken the pressure off me. I don't have to make everyone accountable every Monday morning. He does. It's like having a teacher all over again. He forces me to look at what I'm doing each week to scale my business and what my team is doing to improve their performance. He's been dead honest with me—that he's here to help me get results, and if I don't do it, I simply won't see an improvement in my own business. It's been a long time since I've had that, since I've had to be accountable to someone. It pushes me. It makes me disciplined. It makes my entire team disciplined. And it also takes off the burden a bit of always having to push the train out of the station, because we're all doing it together. It also keeps me from having to rule with an iron fist, which I don't do well. I want people to be friends and happy and all good, which is probably another weakness. Even though people view me as tough, I actually want a lot of joy for everyone I work with, including myself. Bringing in the right person has helped offset all of those weaknesses. I don't think I could have done it without an outside source. That's not a weakness. That's a reality. And because I'm aware of it, I can use outside influences to my advantage. As can you.

Sometimes, though, getting outside help to offset your weaknesses begins with first realizing you have one (or many)—and sharing it with your manager. People who can't see their own weak spots—well, that's red flag number one. So if that's you, do the work to assess where you're struggling. Then articulate it to the people invested in your success, like a business partner, a boss, or a mentor. The most empowering and strong thing about recognizing your own weaknesses and voicing them is that people *respect* you for that. When you can come to that superior—the boss, for example—versus them coming to you, it puts you in a power position. It says you're acknowledging your strengths and weaknesses before they are, which (A) makes them have respect for your self-awareness and (B) makes them want to help you be better. It says you understand yourself.

You can't go waving your weaknesses to your boss like a flag of "know thyself," though. It needs to be done professionally. Set up an in-person meeting so that you have their undivided attention, rather than a phone meeting where who knows what they're doing. Never do it on Monday, because everyone is coming back from their weekend and more often than not they've got a hundred things to do and are less invested in everything else. When you do meet with them, position it as enrolling them in your development plan. Say, "I've noticed that I'm struggling at X, and here's what I'm planning to do about it. Is there anything else you suggest?" Listen and take notes. Then follow up with an email thanking them for their time and outlining the actual steps you both discussed. If I hadn't had this conversation with our president, I never would have gotten the coaching

I needed. Not every weakness requires a coach as a solution, though. You can enroll friends who have strengths you don't. You can take online courses. Watch YouTube videos. Read skill-related books and articles. There's no limit to how creative you can get in order to work on your skills.

AWARENESS AROUND EMOTIONS, TOO

Self-awareness requires not just knowing your strengths and weaknesses but also being in touch with your emotions. Keep in mind that the way you actually feel may have nothing to do with the way you think you *should* feel or wish you felt in any given situation. Learn what your triggers are, even your irrational ones, what motivates you, and what makes you happy. This journey of discovery requires resisting the urge to suppress or change your emotions.

If you do, you risk having an unforeseen moment in a professional situation. You might get triggered by whatever you're suppressing and launch at someone with no idea why you did. If you suppress, you'll eventually blow. In the meantime, it'll make you anxious and unable to think clearly, which causes you to seem disconnected. By bottling up how you feel, you're doing yourself a complete mental disservice that will keep fear in the driver's seat, rather than you.

As I mentioned, this whole "tough bitch" thing comes up a lot for me. For some reason, everyone likes to think that I don't have feelings. As someone once said, just because I carry it well doesn't mean it's not heavy. Maybe it's just more convenient for people to assume that I don't have feelings, I don't know. But honestly, I get so mad when people do that to me, because they don't address the things they need to address.

You have to admit to yourself what you're feeling before you can speak up about it, and you have to do both. It takes courage to admit what you're feeling, because what you're feeling can oftentimes make you vulnerable. I confronted a friend of mine who had posted multiple photos of herself hanging with my ex's girlfriend. When I saw her next, I pulled her aside and said, "Look, this is bothering me and I need to get it off my chest. What you did hurt my feelings, and it made me feel really bad. I need you to know that I am not devoid of feelings, and even though you assume I am tough, remember that I am human, and it hurt." Here's the thing: people are going to make the choices they're going to make. But if they hurt you unintentionally, give them the chance to take accountability for their actions. I've been on the other side of this plenty of times. It shows you know yourself.

Plus, it's action that matters once we identify our feelings. It's not about what we say, what we feel, or what matters to us but about what we do. There's a meme I love: "Don't tell me you miss me. Tell me you are outside with tacos." *Actions.* Being a person who is true to yourself means that you act as such. For yourself and to the people around you. And vice versa. Acknowledge your strengths and weaknesses. Acknowledge your feelings. Acknowledge when you fuck up, and act accordingly.

That girlfriend assumed that I didn't care, and when she heard me out, she immediately appreciated my feelings and apologized. I am glad I said something to her instead of carrying that on my back and building a resentment toward someone I actually like. Plus, if you want to push against people's perception of you, to get them to understand the real you, you have to be willing to show your vulnerabilities. No, that doesn't mean I'm walking around town crying all the time. It means, instead, that when I'm hurt, I say so. When I'm bothered, I express it. When I need to break down, I break down. Walking around with armor all the time would be fucking miserable for everyone, most especially me, because it wouldn't be true.

I recommend continually asking yourself the following questions:

What am I feeling? Try to identify what emotions are running the show.

What do I need here? Get an understanding of what you personally might need.

The more often you ask yourself these questions, the easier it'll be to learn your larger patterns and figure out what you personally require to function, to focus, to succeed, and to be happy.

Once you trust your emotions, it'll be easier to determine your needs, and once you know your needs, it'll be easier to make hard decisions that fly in the face of other people's expectations. Like selling my home in Brentwood. People couldn't believe I was leaving the family home that I raised my girls in over the last decade. It's a gorgeous two-story house designed by architect Steve Giannetti. It was a sanctuary for me.

While there were a lot of great memories there, there was also a heaviness to that place. I felt like in order to emotionally move on from that chapter with my ex, I needed a new house, to start new. Trust me, it required a bunch of difficult conversations, especially with my kids. I knew they needed to see that I was moving on from the divorce. They were on board, but I know they're like me—tough cookies who are sensitive underneath. Decisions don't all feel easy and exciting all the time. Sometimes the right decisions are the hardest ones to act on. They're difficult and emotional and full of friction.

When you know yourself, which includes knowing your needs, you know that those difficulties will be worth it. The decisions become very clear when you're living for what motivates you, not what you fear others will think. You'll be able to tune shit out more. The difference between those who make the right decisions and those who don't is self-awareness. You're the only one who has to live in your body. You're the only one who knows what you actually need. Their perceptions don't mean shit. Your self-awareness does.

Self-awareness *does* get easier. You'll struggle for it. You'll put in the time. And you'll fall on your face. But you've got to make every mistake that you can and never be afraid of taking that chance. Have the wild night even though you need to wake up in two and a half hours, work late and skip the event because you have a project that could put you over the line, put your hat in for the promotion no one thinks you want, or acknowledge that the life you dream of might be different from what your family thinks you need. If you don't live your life, if you never slow down enough to know who you are in your own life, you'll never get to the place of self-awareness. The sooner you're willing to do that, and toss perfection and perception to the side, the easier this is all going to get. You'll live freely, confidently, according to you. And that'll benefit every last room, situation, and conversation that you ever find yourself in. Because you'll have the most important thing—the *real* you. I waited too long to be true to myself. Don't let it happen to you.

Chapter 8

REFOCUS

I had this client, Jackie, who moved across the country and left her beautiful LA home. This was a house with high ceilings, wide hallways, and pretty glamorous decor—at least when it was filled with their big family and all the furnishings. There was so much life and love in that house when they were living in it. But now, without anyone occupying the home, it was proving really hard to sell, because it was a half-empty house and the interiors were really specific to the client. Originally, they used the agent who had sold their last two houses and made an unbelievable profit for them. They thought using this same guy would get them the same outcome. But that didn't prove to be the case, and the house sat on the market forever. It was a lot of property for someone to take on—it was very big and very flawed, and we were chasing the market.

After taking over the listing, reducing the price, and staging the home as best I could, I quickly realized that despite my best efforts to save this, the house was not appealing to the buyer I was hoping for. I had interest only from developers, who historically are the cleanest but also lowest offers. It was miserable for Jackie and, in turn, miserable for me. All she wanted was for me to sell this house for her, but when you're the second or third agent on a property, there's pressure to get it done. And trying to tell your client—who raised her children there, and they loved it so, so much—that no one appreciates it and the only way to sell is to tear it down? That's not a fun convo. Either they had to carry two mortgages for the next two eternities, holding out for their overvalued listing price . . . or they had to trust me to bring it down $2 million and get it sold.

If she had been willing to adjust her perception of the value of her home sooner, and see that things had shifted in the market and chasing it wasn't good for her, we both would have saved ourselves a lot of stress (and money). It's risky to move in a new direction, or it can feel that way. What I've found over the years is that it's actually much riskier *not* to. Don't cling to a choice just because you spent a lot of time making it. If you're willing to take a hard look at what's working and, more important, what's not, and make changes with that information, you'll be moving in the right direction. Taking these risks builds your confidence over time. You'll trust yourself a little bit more. You'll trust that you can make hard decisions (or easy ones) when things aren't working for you. You'll be staying true to yourself, and there's nothing that feels more powerful.

Shit, if you don't choose to refocus . . . you *will* get left behind. It's honestly not as scary as you think. It's like throwing yourself off the diving board—you don't know how deep the water is, but the truth is you've been walking around the pool long enough. It's a calculated risk. At this point, you've got to say, *I'm just going to do this.* No part of my life is off limits to refocusing. When I do my annual reevaluation, I do it across all the areas of my life, because success is never about just one thing, and the confidence you build in one area of your life will impact the others. I ask myself a few questions across five buckets: my work life, my friendships, my family, my dating life, and my health. To make the choice to refocus in these areas, the questions I ask myself are these:

- ***What's not working?***

    You'll notice that your answers will naturally tell you where you're trying to do too much, where you're overacting, and where you're in your own way. That's the beauty of this simple question: the answer will point you to exactly where you already knew you were struggling.

- *Given that, what specific things could I be doing differently?*

These two questions help me understand what events happened in my life this year and what I could do differently next year. This will make me better in all areas. What I've found is that as I've gotten older, I don't have as much time as I once did. So I have to really examine where things *aren't* working and make changes accordingly. I don't mess with what's good. I refocus what's out of sync; sometimes that means pulling back from things, and sometimes that means going all in.

Here's how my annual reevaluation looks right now:

THIS YEAR I HAVE HONED THREE THINGS IN MY BUSINESS THAT COULD BE WORKING BETTER:

- *Team dynamics and leadership*

    I need to make sure that the needs of my team are being met and that people are respectful of each other. I have instituted a three-strikes policy. If I have to have a conversation with you about respect or attitude toward other team members three times, you are out. I hate how black-and-white this policy is, because there is always room for learning through our mistakes, but it takes me out of the position of having to endlessly agonize and analyze whether or not someone is meant to continue. I tend to be loyal to a fault, and by instituting this policy, I am taking myself out of the equation of having to make that decision.

- *Relationships with outside brokers*
  I need to implement a policy that once a week, I will meet another broker for either coffee or lunch to work on developing more relationships. I am realizing more and more that co-listing property can be a very beneficial opportunity for me, considering my schedule and inability to devote myself 100 percent to each client. It's just an impossibility. My new philosophy this year is to go get more co-lists, both in my brokerage but outside my team and outside my brokerage at other companies.

- *Networking with business contacts*
  As if there weren't already enough things in iCal, I am going to implement another weekly meeting with a business contact outside real

estate. I need to be garnering more leads from my biz contacts. By doing another weekly coffee, drink, or lunch, I am creating stronger relationships and forcing them to think of me first, before one of the other hundred agents they know.

SIMILARLY, I'VE FOCUSED IN ON FOUR AREAS OF MY PERSONAL LIFE TO IMPROVE:

- ***More special time with my girls***

  This year is important. We are in a new home where memories and traditions need to be established. So I am going to make sure that every holiday is celebrated and we add two special vacations together to a place we have never been before. I am starting with Thailand.

- ***Staying focused on fitness***

  I made a big effort this year to be more consistent with my workouts, but I do get caught up, and with my schedule, I am not as consistent as I would like to be. It is very easy to get sidetracked, so I am committing myself to five days a week with a trainer to have more accountability. Not solely to look good, but to keep my head screwed on straight.

- *Time with friends is important—missing moments with people important to me*

  I have a hard time with this because I have incredible men and women in my life. But having two jobs, moving, and closing out my chapter with my ex was a challenge this last year. Due to that, I think I have let down a couple of people important to me. So I am going to evaluate the top tier and make sure that they remain close to me. That means less time for myself, which I already have so little of, but I do find that they fill me up, and they deserve the same in return. We are all busy, and many of my besties have called me out on "I am so sorry I haven't checked in for a couple weeks, I have just been slammed." They are over it, and I don't blame them. Work in progress . . .

- *Last but not least—dating*

  Oh, dating . . . how fun and exhausting at the same time. This last year I was open to anything and everything, and sometimes that led me down relationship paths that might be fun but probably less permanent. I think this year I want to focus on dating people who are more aligned with what I really am looking for. That means no more man-children! That is not age specific. Some of the more mature men I have dated have been in their early thirties and not their fifties. What does that say about the men I dated in their fifties? Yikes . . . Well, again, learning curve.

IT'S OKAY TO CHANGE YOUR MIND

Just because you decided you wanted to pursue a career in one area doesn't mean you'll still want that a decade (or even a year) later. I did this with acting in my twenties. For most of my life I had wanted to be an actor—it was a passion, a source of inspiration, and it made me very happy. And before I knew it, I had flipped the switch and gone into real estate. It's hard to say if that was the safe bet or the risky one, but I knew I would be leaving behind one of the greatest things that I loved.

Looking back, I was able to do that only because I got a real-life glimpse into what being an actor was actually like through my dearest friend, Sasha. At the time, I had so many friends who were having small successes on TV shows and pilots. I was going out on random auditions here and there, waiting tables, and working in my dad's office. I was getting a bit disenchanted with acting, because I didn't fit into casting directors' hot-girl mold but wasn't quirky and weird enough to fit into the funny-girl mold either. I was in between. So I thought I needed to get out. I was in that phase of my life where I didn't have the sense of confidence that I have today. I didn't have the sensibility that I would get better and didn't have to fit into either mold, that I could make the mold. I didn't believe in myself enough to believe that at the time. So when my friend Sasha Alexander called me while I was at my dad's office working and hating my life, I grilled her on how amazing it must be. "You're fucking doing it, Sash. You're doing everything we dreamed of. Does it feel like you hit the jackpot?" And her response flipped a switch for me. She said it wasn't what we'd thought. It wasn't one big happy family, and it was a bureaucracy and bullshit on set. Most of it was crazy, and the hours were insufferable. Hearing that from my best friend at the time, hearing that she wasn't happy from hitting the acting jackpot, hit me like a ton of bricks. I figured if she wasn't fulfilled, then I should stop torturing myself on auditions and really evaluate if I wanted to do this.

So I moved toward something that was really energizing to me—real estate. And I'm still constantly doing that. There's no staying static here. If I change my mind, then I change my mind. You don't have to be scared of wanting something new just because it's not what you once wanted.

WHO'S ADDING VALUE

Friendships are a big part of our lives, and if they're not working, it's going to add a bit more stress and fear to your relationships that you simply don't need. Friendships should be a source of strength; friends should be people who build you up or, in the case of my best friend, Tash, act like your bodyguard when you're in a vulnerable part of your life. My friendships have been an area that's required some serious evaluation. Especially with your relationships, it's a never-ending inquiry. I pay close attention to the following:

- Who is adding value to my life, and who isn't?
- Who is sucking the energy from me, the energy I *really* need to be leading any room?
- Who brings me positivity during bad times (like crazy, demanding clients or a heart-wrenching divorce)?

Sometimes you can't control the negativity in a work deal, or with family members, or sometimes even in marriage, but your friends should be nothing but positive. They should be a source of confidence-building energy for you, which is why I always evaluate my friendships before anything else.

Anyone who thinks strife and negativity in female friendships is normal is so wrong. Maybe it's because I'm at a
place where I don't have time for that shit, but I love
women! I want to be around the ones who celebrate me
and celebrate each other, and with whom there's not judgment but rather an understanding that everyone is in their
own process and their own place in their own journey. So
when you refocus, look for friends who advocate for you in
every part of your life and are there to support you no matter what's going on. Are they bringing you positivity? Do
they make you laugh? Do you sense a genuine connection?
If you do, they're in. If you don't, they're done.

The trials of my life have really shown me who my true
friends are. When I went through my divorce, which is
obviously a challenge for any couple (and friend group), it
was a natural turning point that forced me to refocus my
friendships in order to see success outside them. Regardless of how people want to put it, in most cases friends
have to pick sides when the couple splits. There's just no
way around it. There are very few cases of divorce where
someone hasn't done something wrong and everyone re-
mains "besties." For the most part, people pick a side. I
had one friend in particular who has a bit of a reputation
for—how do I say this nicely?—maybe staying closer
friends with only the husbands? I, of course, overlooked
that. I thought this friend was a genuinely lovely person.

She's a homemaker, a caretaker, and is so sweet, kind, and loving. And a killer hostess. There were all of these things that I loved about her and that I really enjoyed. So I overlooked her relationship with my husband. But eventually, I had a few of my true friends sit me down, make me *take a sip*, and let me know a few things. What they shared gave me no choice but to make a hard decision to refocus that person out of my life. I legitimately, very simply, stopped talking to her. I asked a couple of my friends to keep me off the invite list if she was invited so I didn't have to be around her—for the near future, anyway.

It had been a *while* since I had seen this woman, and then just recently I was hosting a work event in Bridgehampton. I had a table of fourteen that I was entertaining and thus networking, when she walked up to the table because she knew a few of the people I was hosting. I made an immediate, instinctual choice in that moment to put my sunglasses on and look the other way. Screw me once, shame on you. Screw me twice, shame on me. So I put my glasses on and iced her out.

Interestingly enough, I thought I was being the mature adult, because the last thing I want to do is have an uncomfortable conversation in a social setting where I'm entertaining people. It's business. What am I supposed to say? "Hey, how ya doing? I haven't talked to you in two years because you're a fucking asshole"? I chose what I thought was the high road. But sure enough, I got a text from a mutual connection who is still friends with her:

The truth is, this text message did give me some pause. I did a mini reevaluation in the moment to consider if I should forgive her. If all of this swirl was worth it. The truth is that she has a history of not having very many girlfriends, and I think there's a reason for that. There are women who are *girl's girls*, and then there are *chicks*. There's

a difference. The women I choose to spend time with celebrate other women. It's so funny, because it's so easy to
tell who's a girl's girl—it's a fucking aura or something—
because a *girl's girl* is willing to encourage and celebrate
other women. She's not judgmental. She respects the journey of her friends. She's 1,000 percent honest with you.
Jealousy doesn't invade. She chooses humor, because if we
can't laugh about the crazy that we're all living every day,
what are girlfriends for? She gets that you're all in different
places, and that's okay. This woman wasn't that. She was
a *chick*. Ultimately, I decided I didn't need to step in shit
twice. I finally just got my shoe cleaned.

I share this story not be salacious but to show you that
refocusing isn't always the easiest thing. People will probably have a problem with it. It might cause confrontation
(or dramatic texts). To be perfectly honest with you, I don't
like confrontation. I really don't. Especially with my friends
and the people I love, I prefer to avoid it. I try to put myself
in their shoes and understand where they might be coming
from. I assume goodwill. But I also am not scared to evaluate if that friend is worth the energy and going to help me
conquer other parts of my life.

When you choose to refocus your friendships, different
situations will require different reactions. I had decided to
confront this person prior to cutting her out of my life. But
when things came to light for the final time, there was no

sense in circling back to *talk* about it. It was time to just shut it down. There was nothing to discuss, and we never spoke again. But there are definitely other cases, like the ones we've talked about in business especially, when someone has the ability to make you feel badly about yourself, or they're hitting you below the belt with their comments or sharing things with people that were to remain in confidence—those things warrant a proactive defense. You've got to stand up, which doesn't have to come from an angry place but rather a very clear place about what you'll no longer tolerate.

When you look at your friendships to see what's not working, look for the women who are by your side. You need them. They help combat fear. They make the crazy a little less crazy. And they'll give you a backbone when you feel like you don't have one of your own. It might be risky to make changes, because, yes, people may push back. But on the other side of staying true to yourself is a deeper sense of confidence that you could have found only by choosing to do so.

THE BUSINESS OF SAYING *YES*

Refocusing doesn't always mean constantly peeling back. Actually, especially in business it can mean giving more, doing more, and saying *yes* like it's your job. Because it is. You should say *yes* to something that feels risky every day. *Every single day*. Because you have to try new things in order to get to new levels. Some days, this risk will be big, like the day you decide to hire someone or to negotiate an offer or to move cities. Other days, this risk will be small (but still matter)—like asking to join a meeting you weren't invited to, meeting someone new, signing up for a new training, or wearing something outside your comfort zone.

A reevaluation can tell us as much about what we should be moving toward as it does about what to be moving away from. Right now, I'm saying a whole lot of yes to investing in myself, to spreading myself too thin, and to creating other opportunities in spaces I've never been in before. Like this book. Sometimes refocusing your career is just that: what can you do more of to get closer to where you want to be? And let the rest fall away. For me, as you saw above, I'm letting go of the agonizing and overanalyzing about keeping people on my team. I'm also letting concerns with perception dissipate—this requires being an unapologetically strong woman on the show and not worrying about whether fans see my soft side. Because I'm pouring money into long-term goals like publishing, hiring a business coach, creating systems and infrastructure, and spending more money on my team, I'll personally make less money than I have in a long time because so much of it is going into expanding. But that doesn't mean that it's not working. It's scary, though, for sure.

WHERE DO YOU GO?

In refocusing, when you generally focus on what's not working, as I try to, it becomes pretty obvious what needs to change. Especially in business, when something isn't working, the numbers will tell you that it's not. Or when things are out of alignment, whether it's something personal or something health related, when you're dropping too many balls, it's easy to feel that. I get it, though; I know that just because something's not working doesn't mean you know what will. And you're sorta left with, *Okay, but where do I go, then?* I feel this the most in dating. But you might feel it elsewhere. It doesn't really matter what area of your life it shows up in; it's helpful to feel like you have clarity on the next step that you're taking.

Young people, especially, get so paralyzed by this. You want to know so badly where it's all going, and you so glamorize what it'll look like when you get there, that you don't take a hot second to figure out if it's really for you.

Refocusing means letting yourself change. When you're wondering which fork in the road to take and what you should move toward, it's okay to process and allow yourself that moment of fear. If you know one way might very well lead directly somewhere, and another way is super interesting but it's unclear where it's headed, I'll take the latter route every time. Life is about pursuing what's interesting. Not what's certain. You have to learn how to leave your fear of the outcome behind, especially if you want to shift your focus and find the next phase of yourself and your life. Living in the past, where there's regret and resentment over your choices, is fucking pointless. Likewise, living in the future and the unknown will annihilate you. So all you can really do is to make choices about right now and right here.

My dad used to always say, "Anyone working past five p.m. isn't working right." I work 24/7, so obviously I didn't heed this advice, but his point is that whatever you do, do that at the time and just that. It helps you stay focused and in the flow. And when we're in times of refocus, it's a good sentiment to remember, so that when you get to these very overwhelmed moments, you don't do what you're tempted to do—burn it all down and walk away. When I feel this way I know I need to just take a beat. There will always be highs and lows in life. The lows don't mean we should walk away from it all.

You've got to be prepared to roll, rather than living in the fear of it always being this way. You let the frustration run through you, maybe complain about it, and pivot. Everyone needs a minute to relook at their life. Whether it's a weekend away or going out with a girlfriend and having twenty-five margaritas or getting a massage. When you have the moments where you're hitting a huge wall and don't know what direction you're even headed in, you have to recognize that pushing into bigger rooms means high-stress situations where you'll lose sometimes. It's important to honor those feelings of *Fuck, I don't want to do this anymore*, and let them flush through you. Remind yourself who you are, breathe, baby girl, refocus, and try again.

Chapter 9

....

KEEP IT
MOVING

Y ou're going to experience failure over and over again, especially as you're reaching for more of what you want. Worrying about failing doesn't making failing easier. You need to leave your fear in the back of your closet, stuffed next to that bad trendy skirt that you never should have purchased to begin with. Failure is inevitable if you're pushing forward. In my business (and my life, if we're being totally honest), whenever I don't win a listing, I feel it. It's that little twinge of *Fuck, I don't want to do this anymore.* When things go south for me (which, believe me, happens *a lot*), sometimes I want to give up. Because I'm tired and/or burnt out, emotionally and physically exhausted. The fear that things won't get better, or that you're not doing enough, or that you're letting down the people that matter . . . it'll get you. That's why you can't sit around and wallow in what's happening. You have got to keep it moving.

The past few years I've had to keep it moving. I had no choice. Every time I wanted to give up, I remembered that I had a lot of people to prove wrong. Look, last year was a terrible year, and I'm not afraid to admit it. There were a lot of things happening at once. I took a huge hit in my business because I brought on a partner, and the market wasn't exactly great. While I was trying to keep things above water there, I was divorcing my husband, breaking up our family, and trying to still have some semblance of a personal life. I drank a lot of tequila last year. Who are we kidding? This year, too, but for different reasons. Or one reason—my client Jeff. More on that later.

When fear is dominating your day, or even your year, if you keep moving, most people won't be the wiser. I can't tell you how many people thought I was doing *really* well. They didn't see me on my back patio, lighting up cigarettes and crying to myself or to my best girlfriends. When I was winning business or taping my show or showing up to a social event, they saw exactly what I wanted them to see, which was someone who was moving forward and not looking back. You can be a complete and utter wreck, you can be drowning in anxiety and everything can be going wrong, but if you want to command respect and get yourself out of the hole that inevitably happens to all of us as we're taking on bigger rooms, more success, and different personalities, you'll have to find a way to keep pushing forward. There's just not room for *Woe is me* when things aren't going your way. (Trust me, I want to bitch as much as the next person. Do it for a hot second and get going.)

When I walked through the door of my office or into a party, people saw only what *I* wanted them to see. I projected that calm energy. It was very rare that I would ever lose it in public. I'm not scared to show my weaknesses (or I wouldn't be telling you this), but when it comes to business, you've got to be careful. You've got to compartmentalize and keep it moving if you want to show up in a room and command respect. When you get burned or go through tough stuff, you've got to just chalk it up to what it was, put your best foot forward, and move on to the rooms you're meant to be in.

DON'T STOP UNTIL YOU'VE LIVED TO TELL ABOUT IT

People will be betting on your weakness. They'll plan to take advantage of it. But if you follow the advice in this book, you'll come out on top, because you'll see their power plays coming a mile away. And you'll know how to push back when you can, fight back when you need to, and endure when you're tired. I learned the strength of my own backbone with one client I battled to land, then persisted through misery working for, and I've since circled back years later to see the battle through by pursuing her in a commission dispute. Every once in a while, selling someone's greatest asset—their home—will bring out the absolute worst in a person. My client Jane was one of those people, and it made my life an absolute hell. She had bought two properties on the Westside for $2 million each. She was going to do one on spec and sell it and keep one for herself. I was up against two or three really good brokers to get this listing.

When I got the call about who she was considering going with, she said it could be me if I lowered my commission to 1.5 percent to match the other broker. In that moment, I had to make a choice to fight for it. I told her if she wanted to hire someone at a discount, that was what she was going to get—discount quality. She pursued me a little further and we settled on 2 percent, noting that we would have other opportunities to work together, as this was not her last project. I knew her tough nature, and I knew she wouldn't respect me if I took it at 1.5 percent. So I fought. And I fought respectfully. This was a defining moment when, with my experience, I should have seen what was coming. A 1.5 percent commission on a deal like this is a no-no. You'll see why.

There were signs along the way, red flags that I chose to look past. I wanted in on the developer business she was working on, and if taking a little shit from her was a part of the deal, then so be it. Basically, if she was going to be buying up and developing properties for huge numbers, I wanted to be her go-to agent. Turns out, my team couldn't do anything right. No matter how many open houses we had, we didn't market them enough or not enough buyers came through to please her. She was perpetually unsatisfied and would call and yell at me about how much we were screwing up for her. I mean, if I could insert her voice right now, I would: "Traeee, listen, Trae, you have got to get more buyers through the door. . . ." She would find fault with anyone she worked with on her home—construction companies, designers, electricians, painters, even the stagers were beaten up on their fees. She expected 110 percent but only wanted to pay 50 percent.

But I had fought so hard to get her listing that I continued to persist through her abuse. I was overworked, exhausted, and underappreciated. But I kept saying to myself, *I fought like shit to get this. I have to sell it. Do not let her fire you.* I had been up against such impressive and notable agents—and beat them—that I didn't want to turn around and lose it.

Here's where things get really interesting. While I was trying to sell this $8 million property for her, I concurrently took over the sale of her condo on Wilshire Boulevard, which was a $2.5 million listing that she had on the market with another agent. She had the listing at a crazy price, almost $1 million more than it would end up going for. Over the course of nine months, we had super low offers that were closer to the price I thought it should have been listed at to begin with. When our contract to work on that condo expired, I knew she would go back to "for sale by owner" because she was so committed to getting an extra $100,000 that no one could tell her anything she didn't want to hear (like the trades that were happening because our buyers were moving on other properties, which happened at least twice). In other words, we were losing buyers to other listings in the neighborhood because she refused to negotiate on price. I had done everything for this woman on *this* listing, too, even fluffing up her staging with things from my own personal home. At every touch point with Jane, I was going above and beyond. We had gotten a couple different offers; the first was contingent on the sale of the buyer's other condo, which was in escrow at a really good price, and the other was from a tenant in Jane's building. At the end of the listing period, I hadn't sold it, but I delivered an exclusion list that was a mile long and included the people we had been in escrow with.

Per the contract, when you deliver an exclusion list, it means that for a certain number of days, the client can't sell their home to someone on the list; otherwise they must still pay you your commission. Well, when Jane *did* close on her house before the exclusion list expired, it was with the same buyer that we had put under contract. Representation on both sides were removed from the deal in an off-market transaction. *Oh, shit . . . here we go.* Now, during this time, I was representing her $8 million property still, so I remained silent and simply inquired about the sale to understand if it was a buyer that was on my exclusion list. She avoided the question and responded saying how lucky she was to have a neighbor who had come to her and that she had been able to close it. When I inquired who, she said, "These people across the hall." I desperately wanted to give her the benefit of the doubt. No one could be that shady. But she didn't come clean. I spoke with the original buyer's agent that we were in contract with and said that my client had stated that it was a neighbor across the hall, and at this point I had to report this to management and allow them to investigate further before I pursued any confrontation.

When the listing period on the $8 million property was coming to an end and I knew I was probably getting released from that (she'd probably think that was the safest way to get away from me), I fought like hell to keep the listing and add a co-list agent from another company who was doing a lot of business in the area and was/is a great colleague of mine. I convinced the client that she was getting me, who knew the house better than anyone, and a new agent with a fresh perspective for the same price. Because of that I was able to maintain that listing, and within the next few months, we closed it and I moved on. Well, from that listing.

Once management reviewed my file and the time line and public record on the closing of the Wilshire property, my company wanted to formally file a commission claim and go for mediation. Without getting too far into the details, she *had* been in contract with someone on my exclusion list when she wasn't allowed to be. I knew I had her.

There were several attempts to settle the commission dispute, and she ignored our requests for over a year. Finally, with our attorneys going back and forth, we settled on a mediation date, which took place two weeks ago as I write this. From 10:00 a.m. until 6:00 p.m., we went back and forth with a mediator. I had hundreds of emails and backup documentation supporting my claim, and she had nothing in writing supporting hers. After eight hours, at 6:01 p.m., she agreed to pay the commission owed to me. I had successfully fought and won.

I am so glad I saw it through to the end. I had to fight for what was right, despite the fees and hours spent preparing the documents and file. It was worth it, because I was not going to allow her to do this to me or someone else. I believe wholeheartedly that she did not think I had the stomach for the mediation and that if she dragged it out long enough, I would just give up. I hung in there and I am proud that I did. There are certain things you don't look forward to, like mediating a divorce, but in this case I wanted the statement to be made formally that I would not be walked on, and lucky for me, I had the full support of my company behind me.

When you are persistent, it means that you're sticking with it when things are hard. If life were easy, persistence wouldn't be what differentiates the strong from the weak. Certain things you just have to actually live through. You have to sometimes live through rejection and verbal abuse, taking hours of terribly difficult personalities. You'll cry (I did). You'll wonder why the hell you're doing this (same). You'll have people who are toxic and negative. But when you see these situations through, you're developing your gut and inner strength. This is so much of what makes any business, especially mine, anything but glamorous. It's downright difficult. Sales is dog-eat-dog, because no one makes a salary here. Everyone is operating from a place of survival, and some people will do whatever it takes (like playing dirty), and when you're on the receiving end of "whatever it takes" that's where you learn the real life lessons on what's worth it. And what's not. And how to make that decision the next time around.

WHEN THE SHIT HITS THE FAN

Here's the truth—when you continue to find ways to push past your own fear, it means you'll be pushing toward some serious success. That's the whole point. But when you do that, it also means the stakes get incredibly high. I've seen this in the last four years: I'm firing on all cylinders all the time, but that also means there's so much more to lose. The pieces of real estate I'm representing have extra zeros on their prices now. The clients are more high-profile. There are more eyeballs on every damn thing I do. There are more demands on my time. It's all elevated, and this is what I asked for! So when the shit hits the fan, it's ten times messier than it was a few years ago.

And when it *does* hit the fan (because it will), you get to freak out. But then you have got to get cleaning. I learned this lesson loud and clear last week. My team was managing a full reveal of one of the more expensive listings of my career—with my client Jeff. This reveal was so much more than a launch to me; it was a chance to prove myself. I wanted everyone to be proud of me (don't we all?). And I didn't want to make a misstep—not for myself, not for the client, not for my team. It was our time to show this demanding client what we were made of. It needed to go *per-*

fectly. We'd been giving it 150 percent of our attention so that it would.

It did not go perfectly. Not even close. Part of this launch included a major piece of press that we'd been working on with the publication's editor all week. The information was embargoed, meaning absolutely nothing could go out publicly until a certain time. We'd done the interview, cross-checked all the facts about the listing, managed Jeff's feedback on how he felt the interview went, and tried our best to work with the publication to make this press as splashy as it could be. I was basically playing real estate broker, talent manager, publicist, and god knows what else for weeks—and I was at my breaking point.

So it did not make for a pretty scene when the press team told me that the article went live *without* our revisions to the property specs and without my client's approval. Jeff had said, "Absolutely nothing goes out before I fact-check it. You must make sure that I get to fact-check this." When our PR people sent me the three or four questions that they called "fact-checking," I called Jeff and was going over that on the phone, but he was off on some tangent that went longer than it should have.

As we were on the phone, PR called to tell me the publication had posted the piece. I had told them over and over again that nothing could go out last minute because of how obsessed my client was with having approval over *everything.* I started screaming at the press team, telling them to *get it taken down NOW.* I completely lost my shit. I yelled at them for what probably felt like an eternity. I was panicked trying to understand why the piece had gone live without any of our changes. I completely lost control, because I was so scared of this going wrong, of looking bad, and of this difficult client handing me my ass. I knew I was about to get verbally beat up over this, so in turn I was doing the same to the people around me. It was really out of character for me, and luckily the people I lost it with are people I trust. My blowup was all in house, but that's still a big, scary thing to have happen—to feel like you're out of control in a scenario because you're so fearful of an outcome. I had to gather myself big time. Luckily, my partner, Gina, brought me back down so we could move forward.

Thank god, because when we got summoned by the angry client to his office, I was a total mess, and I think my team was genuinely concerned for my well-being. The best thing I did that day was let Gina make the plan for our meeting. She had to take control, because I'd lost my ability to control the room anymore. Fear was controlling me. She had to take over so I had time to gather myself once the meeting began progressing. She showed up to this meeting with paper samples and collateral that had his name and brand all over them. She knew that the best way to get him out of his head was to focus on something other than his perceived anger at my "fuckup." I had such nervous energy going into that meeting, I would have been way too reactive. Reacting is fine if you stay in control, as we talked about, but I had lost my ability to do that. Having a partner who was there for me was a huge asset, and we got through the meeting without anyone (especially me) losing it. But it was a close call.

I had such a physical reaction to this meltdown, because of the pressure and the anxiety of it all. I'm sharing this with you because what came next is the important part. These meltdowns happen all the time (okay, hopefully not all the time, because that's just bad, but you're not going to get through your career without them), but when they take over your entire state of being, as they did mine, it's what you do next that counts. And whether it's a product-launch meltdown or the meltdown of a marriage (we'll get to that), it's the moments and days afterward that will determine whether you win. Or not.

I had to have a conversation with myself that went something like this: *You're either going to let this take you down today, or you're going to need to flip the switch and keep moving on.* That's what I did. Because even after the toughest of days, like when I was fighting with my husband and crying over our future apart, or when I was on the verge of a nervous breakdown like this one over a huge business deal going wrong, I know that the next day is a new day. Luckily, the next day for me was the perfect thing to flip the switch. Shooting for *Million Dollar Listing Los Angeles* got canceled, so I sat for six straight hours and just focused and had some quiet time. I was able to come back down and get recentered to remind myself of my power. I was silent, because as loud as I can be and as vocal as I am (I'm a fighter; you scream at me and I'm going to scream back louder), I needed a full day to figure out what I could do to feel like myself again. What could I do to keep moving that would move me past the fear that was weighing me down?

DO OTHER WORK

When you're all twisted up in the fear and intensity and anxiety of a situation, sometimes you'll want to dive deeper into it. We're masochists like that. We dig ourselves deeper and deeper into this quicksand of worry by focusing on nothing other than the situation at hand, when actually what we need to do is something, anything else entirely. When all my freak-out feelings had finally subsided, and our terrible meeting that the client called in order to lay into me was over, I knew I'd need to concentrate on other things. This can be hard, but you've got to do it. You can't let the fear and anxiety keep you right where they want;

you've got to push to new places by doing basically anything at all.

What did I do? I loaded pictures for another listing to a Dropbox folder. It was so junior-assistant of me and something I probably haven't done for my business since I was twenty-eight years old. I wasn't sure why I was doing it at the time, but looking back, I needed something small and mundane to do that could immediately remind me on some level that I was valuable and that I could manage a situation with full authority, even if it was a friggin' upload. When you're out of control, that's kinda what you've got to do. If you can find any type of work that makes you feel in control of your outputs and your emotions again, on some level it will make you feel like you're righting the other wrong. And it'll work. It'll get you out of your head. I was uploading pictures because I knew that it was something I could do without oversight, or being micromanaged, or any potential for being screamed at by my client. It was mundane, but it was something small that could get my head space out of that situation.

And when I woke up, it was time to do more of the same. I needed to sit down and focus on the entirety of my work, not just this one personality and one situation that were dominating my fears. So I got to work checking in on other clients. I had six hours of uninterrupted time grinding, where I didn't have to be running around or getting dressed or giving interviews, which allowed me to remember there's more to my career and my success than this one overwhelming situation.

When you get hyperfocused on one personality or one situation, you'll get derailed. There will always be road bumps and meltdowns and complete psychos that show up on your path. There will be a few crazies, no doubt. But there's value in being able to shift and in reminding yourself that you *have* to shift. Shift your mind-set. Shift your tone. Shift your whole being. Doing other work is a great way to get into that shift, especially when you're coming off something super intense. You simply can't let the rest of your relationships or your life or your business crumble. You don't want one person or one road bump to be the reason you lose yourself or lose your other business. They're just not worth it. Most things aren't, even if it feels that way at the time.

So when you're coming off a really tough situation that's supercharged with emotion, find something immediate and small that needs to be done. I don't care if it's washing your dishes, folding the laundry, organizing your in-box, or uploading pictures. If you have control over it and it needs to be done, do it. It'll get your energy going again, and before you know it, you'll be ready to focus on something that actually requires your concentration and intellect. Control what you can control without a tremendous amount of brainpower. You need to do that stuff so you can just not think about the thing you're so badly stressing about. Distract yourself. And if you don't have anything to distract yourself with, I have plenty of photos for you to upload.

Then find the other meaningful work that needs your attention. I pick up on other clients when one client is going south, to remind me that there's an entire body of business to attend to. Think about maintaining a garden: if you only obsessed over the one fucking flower that was wilting and abandoned, you might get that flower to bloom but you'd lose the rest of the garden. Don't do that. Focus on the broader stuff at play. Other colleagues, other relationships, other projects, other problems, other ideas. Do something about those. Call on leads. Text a girlfriend. And whatever you do, don't verbally recount the situation that melted down to every one of your friends. It'll keep you in that crazy energy, rather than letting you move past it.

STFU

I can out-talk the best of them. But part of keeping it moving is keeping it moving forward. If you spend all of your time talking about a situation that you're freaking out about or a failure that's haunting you, and you dissect it with literally every person you meet, you'll simply never move forward.

Knowing ahead of time who are my go-to people (and for what situations) has been really helpful when I'm confused or fearful or unsure. Because everyone has their own perspective. Some people lead with advice from their heart, and some people lead with their mind. When you're uncertain about something or about how to move forward, those two things are playing tug-of-war, and if you open yourself and what's confusing you to too many people, you lose yourself. I don't care what the fuck it is; getting 450 opinions on whether or not you should get a divorce or quit working for that abusive boss or take that job and move across the country or how you should handle your stress from a terrible situation . . . After taking in all those opinions by talking to every single one of your friends, you're not more clear than when you started asking for them.

It's important to make a plan ahead of time, to know which people will help you move forward in which situations. Here are a few types of people I think are integral in helping you solve different problems. These are the ones that come up the most in my own life. If you can take a minute to figure out who's the most helpful in these areas, you'll be better able to limit how much you're talking about a situation. Here are some questions to help you figure out which person might be best for what situation, because I find that in our personal life and our business life, we're dealing with either issues or decisions. The issues are the *shit that's hitting the fan*, the meltdowns, the messes. The decisions are the actions we need to take, the places we need to go, the dreams we have, and the things we need to do next.

Who can you show your dark side to? We all have one. We all need someone in our life we can show all the parts of ourselves to. It's good to know who this person is because they're likely the one who won't judge. They won't judge you for how you yelled at someone. They won't judge you for the rant you go on, saying a lot of things you don't mean about the person you're dealing with. They'll hear you and then move you back to the real issues and your real self—the person deep down who doesn't actually mean all those things. I am lucky to have a few, for when one gets tired of my shit. Lol.

Which of your friends is the best listener? These are the people who can help you pull out or see your own answers. Listeners are clutch in many of life's big moments, especially the listeners who really get you because they've seen you through so many of life's ups and downs. Match that with some good listening skills, and you have the perfect person to run things by. Especially when you're trying to solve for what the right decision is in your personal life or relationships.

Who understands the type of work you do, whom you trust implicitly? You gotta talk to someone who *gets it*. Gets you. And won't run their mouth. We need these people in our business and careers, because they'll act as sounding boards and be able to provide sound thoughts on what to do now and what to do next. But you have to remember that sometimes this isn't a partner or team member because they would be too close. It could be a friend at another company, an executive you respect, or even a business coach.

Who has a business or career that you admire, whom you can call at a moment's notice? The people in your world whom you really respect, and who are also close to you, are good people to call on when you're facing a fork in the road.

They'll be people with a take on your situation that you actually care to hear. It's singular input that may or may not work for you, but it'll be a good outside opinion, and one that you respect.

Whether you could answer these questions with a handful of people or a single person, the number doesn't matter. All that counts is that you know who your people are, and you keep your problem solving and venting to those people alone. Regardless of who you end up going to, you have to find the answers to combat your own fear within yourself. You have to find your answers to decisions about what to do through you and only you, and maybe some rosé. Talking to the one person who knows you and actually understands what you're dealing with and what you've been through can provide good food for thought. Opinions are like assholes: everybody has one. So be forewarned before running your mouth all over town. All that these opinions will do, especially when they're unqualified (as in, they don't *really* know you, get you, etc.), is complicate your instincts. That's the most important thing to remember before sharing your shit with *everyone* in an effort to feel better. It won't make you feel better. It'll make you feel worse, and you'll be no closer to moving beyond it than you were before. You don't want people guiding you down paths that are more about them than they are right for you.

This way, you'll be able to own your decision, right or wrong. You'll be able to own your reality, good or bad.

MOVE UNTIL THE END, AVOID THE SPLINTERS

Sometimes, in order to keep your life moving forward, you have to move past. And that'll require moving on from people completely and letting them go and out of your life. Look, moving on is not my strong suit. So you're learning from someone who's worked (and is working) really hard to learn this lesson myself. I think the most important lessons are often the hardest ones to learn (ugh, I know). I'm loyal as hell, and I'm very passionate, and when I see something in someone and I care, it takes me a really long time to get to the place where I just move on. I'm loyal to people even if they've shit on me from time to time. It takes me longer than most to let people go and out of my life. It's probably one of my greatest weaknesses, and it shows up in all different parts of my life.

But if you sit on the fence and wait and rethink and deal with the BS and wonder some more, want to know what will happen? You'll get fucking splinters in your ass. You've got to get yourself to a place where you recognize that you're staying in a situation too long and that you're not moving forward at all. You're not doing anything about it. You're just living in fear of what's next, or what people will think, or what will happen.

I already know that with my client Jeff, I'll tap that relationship out here soon, because there's only so much one person can take. But I'm not there yet, for whatever reason. And I'm going to get splinters. I mean, for sure I already have them. Recognizing that you're not moving forward or doing anything about the fear you're living in is part of the puzzle. At least you know. Once you are indeed done, and you're ready to move on and move forward (that may take me a long time; I basically require someone to push me off the fence), you will.

I've had so many situations where I didn't get moving until I almost didn't have a choice, where I was very unfulfilled. Some people are very defined in their boundaries, and I can totally talk a good game because I can intellectualize the hell out of anything. So I'll ride situations until the bitter end. Until I'm so burnt out by the situation that there's just no coming back. Some decisions are actually worth that much energy. Some are not.

But take it from someone who's sat on this fence too long too many times: if a situation makes you want to get back under your covers, or keeps you from concentrating, or paralyzes you with indecision and fear, then something has to change. That's when you know you've got to get off the fence, when you stop being able to compartmentalize it and instead it's basically a companion to every second of your day. If you're failing at compartmentalizing, it probably means that it's time to move on.

Plus, it's difficult to not bring that stress into the people and the relationships that you're the most comfortable around. Those people deserve your good energy, not just scraping-the-barrel energy.

ONWARD

As you're learning to trust your gut more and more, and tune in to what pulls you away from those instincts, you're going to find so much freedom in your choices. It doesn't mean that fear will go away, but you'll have a better relationship to yourself and to your own life. You'll know better how to pull which parts of you into any situation, based on the fight you're taking on, or the personality in front of you, or whatever the hell it is that you're trying to accomplish. You'll start feeling like there's absolutely no one to blame but yourself, and even that will include compassion because you know you're at least trying. It's the most empowering feeling in the world to know that fear *finally* isn't running your life, but rather you are. It's what gives you the backbone that only true, self-sourced confidence can.

Owning your truth, your confidence, and your life will draw people to you. It's such a rare quality—not to blame, not to make excuses, and not to play small—that you'll find people enchanted by your power. Life is full of unknowns. There will be plenty of days that you wake up feeling like shit from having made a bad decision or said the wrong thing. You'll never get it 100 percent right. But instead of going into a shame spiral and staying there, you'll be able to leave the past in the past so that you can be accountable to each new day. It'll be the best part of taking on the day and leaving all the fear—of what people think, of not being enough, of where this is all going, of fighting for what you know is right, of failure—behind. Instead, keep moving. Keep staying true to yourself while you do, and you'll own every room you're in.

Acknowledgments

....

First and foremost, I want to thank my family for being my baseline for where my crazy comes from. I would not be the woman writing this book today if each of you hadn't—at different points in my life—given me the encouragement I needed to take the chances I have taken that have landed me here today. To the two beautiful young women I am raising, Juliet and Scarlett—you make my heart burst every day with pride. From the moment you were born, I was changed forever. I feel an immense sense of responsibility raising little girls in today's world. But I am no longer worried about the women you will become. You are both independent, strong, young females who will pave their own path, and I will sit back and watch with such pride. By definition, we aren't a conventional family, but that is what gives us character, grit, and compassion. Raising you both has been my greatest joy in life, and I look forward to watching your journeys, wherever they may take you. I know it is going to be supremely fantastic.

Dad, your sheer and commanding presence growing up is a big part of the success I have had in this crazy business. You raised me to be a fierce female, and look where I am now. You taught me about grit without even saying a word, but you also were there to save the day when I needed you the most. You were my white knight and protected me from getting pummeled so many times that I cannot count. But you also allowed me to make mistakes and learn from them. Simply put, I would not be the boss bitch I am today without you. I know you hate when I curse, but you are a big part of why I am where I am. I am successful. I am independent. I am happy. And as far as the cursing goes, let's just say the apple doesn't fall far from the tree. Just skip over those parts, okay?

Mom and Horst, your absolute, unwavering support and love has been something that I have taken for granted in the past, and writing this book reminded me how I got here. You both have such a massive amount of love in your hearts, and watching you raise my niece Kate has been one of the greatest pleasures in my life. I am so enamored by your passion for life and laughter and love for each other. When things have not been great in my life, you have consistently been there. You have let me cry on your shoulder, told me to get over myself and on with myself, taught me about holding someone accountable, told me I needed therapy when I didn't, and most definitely walked me through the door when I did. You taught me that worthwhile things don't come easy and to always stretch myself beyond what I think is my limit. Most of all you have loved me beyond anything I could imagine. Horst, I already have an incredible father, but you have filled my life with more love and support than I could ever ask for. I am eternally grateful to you. Mom, we laugh, cry, scream, cuss, and live as honestly as we can as a family. The authenticity that I hope comes across in this book and on my show is 100 percent because of you. I hope you know that. We might not be anyone's picture of a perfect family, but I think we fucking rock. So cheers to you, matriarch. I celebrate you.

Kristin, my sister, we have been through this crazy ride for forty-plus years together. We have done some things that I cannot write about (lol), but it's that history and connection, fights and makeups, crying because we're laughing so hard and mostly making fun of our ridiculous family that keep us always coming back to our north. Thank you for picking me up and caring for me when I needed it the most and loving me unconditionally. Thank you for also pushing me emotionally to be braver and live my truth. This life is always changing and evolving, and I am so glad that we have each other on this complicated and amazing journey. Always remember that no matter how pissed you get at me, I will always jump in front of a bus for you, push a chick out of the cab in Sun Valley, or stand between you and any adversary and intimidate them without even a word.

To my extended "framily"—you know who you are—I couldn't do what I do without you all. The busier we become, I am reminded how much you all mean to me, and the laughter that you bring to my life I could not live without. I have known some of you since high school and others for only a few years, but I am consistently in awe of all of you. You have brought me to my knees with laughter and you picked me up when I have been down. You all have encouraged me to go for every opportunity I share, and thankfully you are my biggest fans. You have *never* judged me but only supported me. We spend holidays together, travel together, and celebrate marriages, homes, babies, boyfriends, husbands, and, for some of us, divorces. I couldn't do it without you guys. You are my lifeline and keep me sane and crazy at the same time.

Special love to my ride or die, Natasha. You are my protector and fiercest ally. When I was at my rock bottom, you were right next to me holding my hand. You celebrate me as I am even though at times I can be a little extra or sometimes a lot. You have called me out when I was blowing it and made me a better friend. You have hugged me when I clearly needed it and given me a cigarette only when absolutely necessary. We have been through it the last seventeen years, but we had each other. Honey, you poured the rosé and squeezed the grapefruit when all else had failed us. What else can I ask for in a girlfriend? I have immense love for you, sister, and simply wouldn't do this life without you.

To all the very patient people who made the publishing of this book possible: my entire team at UTA—Max, JB, JT, and especially Brandi Bowles. Your belief in my ability far outweighed my reality, so thank you for challenging me. My editor, Leah Trouwborst, for your support throughout the process. This was completely out of my comfort zone, and I am so lucky to work with you. Finally, Maxie McCoy, you are a badass female, and working alongside you has been such a pleasure. I trusted you implicitly and you never let me down. Thank you for understanding me the way you do, helping me deliver on days that I didn't have anything left to give, and ultimately bringing my voice to this book the way you have.